Living, Laughing and Loving Thru Marriage

by
Finbarr M. Corr, Ed.D.

A humorous guide for couples contemplating marriage and for those already married, whether 7 or 70 years,

filled with personal anecdotes to entertain and educate the reader

FMC Press
P.O. Box 1485
East Dennis MA 02641

First Edition Copyright @ 2006 by Finbarr M. Corr

Cover Design by Janine Myer, Alphagraphics,
Morristown N.J.

Design consultant, John Francis Bourke,
New York N.Y.

Cover photo by Yellow Dog Productions/Photographers
Choice RF/Getty Images

Printed in the United States of America by
Whitehall Printing Company, Naples, Florida

FMC Press
ISBN 1-58570-114-9

Dedication and Acknowledgements

Having spent over 30 years as a marriage and family therapist in New Jersey, and being myself happily married to Laurie for almost 18 years, I felt motivated to share my many professional experiences and personal anecdotes. I want to help married couples, both young and old, to grow in their relationships and have a lot of fun in their marriages. I have been concerned about the lack of marital preparation, the increasing number of marital breakups and the number of people who choose to just live together, possibly too scared to make a lifelong commitment.

Writing a book requires a lot of cooperation and support from different individuals. My writers' group on Cape Cod, headed by John Prophet, has been both challenging and supportive. My editor Mary Woodward has been extremely patient and supportive. Her husband, Bob Woodward, has once again been the architect in formatting and guide in its production. Gina Andreozzi's technical assistance is deeply appreciated. My busy book agent Pierre Lehu, has been both affirming and creative in his suggestions about content and marketing.

More than anyone else, the one person who has been my advocate, loving critic and friend through one more book is my beloved wife Laurie and that is why I am dedicating *Living, Laughing and Loving thru Marriage* to her.

Table of Contents

Prologue

My old English teacher at St Patrick's Cavan, Father Bob McCabe, is turning in his grave again as I start writing another book. "Relax Father I haven't called myself a writer yet. I am just a motivator." I am like so many people who want to be part of something larger than themselves.

A young friend of mine from Dublin, who is raising his children in New Jersey, told me after reading my last book, *A Kid From Legaginne,y* that he has resolved to go home to Ireland at least once a year to visit his parents as long as they are living. He was motivated by the story of my going over to Ireland each Christmas to spend time with my dad after my Mom passed away.

A young waitress from Ireland working on the Cape, also having read my recent book asked, "Finbarr when are you going to tell us the rest of the story about the "kid?" I must confess that I did leave many readers of *A Kid From Legaginney* in the woods, so to speak, because I did not tell how and when I resolved the issue of mandatory celibacy for Catholic priests. How did an Irishman who loved the priesthood resign, get married and get on with his new life? If you are prepared to wait a few months, *Bridges from Legaginney* will be on the shelves of local bookstores.

Just as the "*Kid*" had subtle messages of motivation, *Living Laughing and Loving thru Marriage* will have not so subtle messages for those who are married, those who plan to marry, and those in nontraditional relationships. You too can have a great marriage, but like Tiger Woods becoming possibly the world's greatest golfer ever, it doesn't happen automatically. It takes years of practice and revision of your swing. And when you feel you have it down perfectly, you need to start working at it all over again.

Why am I writing anyway? I don't understand it totally myself. Abraham Maslow wrote years ago, "A musician must make music, an artist must paint, a poet must write if he is to be ultimately at peace with himself. What a man can be, he must be"

Writing for me starts with emotions, and then I organize my feelings and thoughts. I feel at one with you, the reader. I don't mean to talk down to people or be boastful. I sincerely want all of us who believe in marriage, or in any type of committed relationship, not to take it for granted but rather to nurture it with conversation, shared feelings and plenty of laughter.

Chapter 1
What do <u>you</u> bring to the marital bed?

Charlene came into my office some years ago looking for divorce counseling. She had been married to Harry for 25 years. They were incompatible culturally, spiritually and socially. After a few counseling sessions I asked Charlene, "Why did you ever marry Harry?"

"He was a very good dancer." She added with a little grin, "I should have listened to my dad when he said to me on the way to church for the wedding, 'Charlene, I can turn the car right here and drive home if you have any doubts that Harry will be a good husband, because I do.'"

Other clients have told me similar stories over the years, some more humorous than Charlene's. Mike told me a story of having a nightmare in which he was logging wood in a fast flowing river. He was doing okay for awhile, bouncing from log to log as the wood was flowing down the river. All of a sudden he slipped and imagined he was going to be crushed between two logs. He decided to sit on one log and plant his feet firmly on the other. He started pushing with all his might, only to discover suddenly that he had pushed his wife of 40 years out of the bed!

Over breakfast the next morning he confessed to her that he was very frustrated, as nothing he did in the marriage seemed to be good enough. With a little encouragement form his honey, he decided to come for counseling and learn a more rational way of communicating with her.

I have enjoyed working with married couples over the years, but my real passion has been challenging engaged couples to live a joyful, fulfilling marriage. I used to receive some strange looks, especially from the prospective husbands, when I would say, "Marriage is meant to be fun, and it is up to both of you to work at making each day a positive experience by not taking yourselves too seriously."

Some looked at me as if I had two heads, but by the time we finished the six or seven pre-marriage counseling sessions most of them had changed their attitudes and were looking forward to many fun-filled years ahead. For couples who professed to be active participants in their faith, I included some theological insights that I will discuss later in this chapter.

I will agree at the outset that the career of being a pre-marriage counselor has become more difficult this past 20 or 30 years, as society has developed a cynicism about marriage that is causing many couples to choose alternate life styles. Sociologists might ask, "Why should the institution of marriage be any different than other institutions that are going through revolutions and scandals?"

They might point to once respectable institutions like Enron and Arthur Andersen that have been shattered by greed and dishonesty, rendering the lives and the investment of thousands of employees worthless. Unfortunately (or fortunately!), people of faith expect more of marriage as a religious commitment. We are upset that between 38% and 43% of marriages end in divorce and that the ratio of failures is not significantly less for couples who regard themselves as good Christians.

There is also the growing practice of couples doing what many couples did in primitive cultures. They just decide to live together and have children, ignoring the public commitment to marriage altogether. For many young couples, the religious teaching of the permanence of marriage is problematic.

Let's face the facts. People "get hitched" in marriage for a variety of reasons - to cope with loneliness, to satisfy sexual desires, to have children to create a home and, very often, just to feel secure. The challenge I faced for my more than 25 years as a priest was to persuade engaged couples to look beyond their selfish reasons and see marriage not so much as biological relationship of two people but rather as a path to total fulfillment and the beginning of a journey to wholeness and holiness.

I was conscious all the time that I was asking a lot from these couples. With this approach, there was always the fear of creating the expectation that the marriage would always be perfect, never to experience conflict, disillusionment or disappointment. In a later chapter I will discuss how I taught couples how to resolve conflicts and to prevent dissension by establishing a division of labor and a budgeting program in the home at the very beginning.

I always wanted to have couples set reachable goals, and now that I have been married for 18 years I will gladly share my successes and inadequacies in reaching my own marital goals.

In the 1950s when I was studying marriage as a seminarian in Ireland, the primary purpose of marriage was merely for the procreation of children. One of the more positive highlights of the Second Vatican Council (1962-1965) was that the mutual satisfaction of the couple is on an equal footing with the procreation of children. The marital relationship is now viewed as a covenant of love between husband and wife, reflecting the covenant between Christ and his church as a mirror of God's covenant with the people of Israel.

I am not going to lie to you, nor was I ever that naïve to think that every Christian couple was inspired by thinking of marriage as a covenant of love, but when I went on to develop the concept further. As I described how God's chosen people disobeyed God and failed in their commitment by adoring false gods, couples could identify with making mistakes and asking forgiveness. God forgave His people as they turned back from their evil ways and the covenant continued.

I would look at the engaged couple directly and say, "Since you are both human, you will fail one another and thus have to learn to forgive each other and get on with your marriage."

This made the concept of marriage as a covenant more real for them. One of the more fulfilling rewards was meeting the then-married couples several years later, either at a parish function or in a local restaurant. It was humbling to hear them express their deep appreciation for what the sessions did for them as they went through the most important milestone.

Lisa Cahill, a theologian at Boston College and author of Sex, Gender, and Christian Ethics, proposed that the Second Vatican Council affirmation of the marital relationship as a relationship of love was clearly a positive step, but not without perils. She wrote, "One of the potential downsides of this however is that one of the reasons for divorce today is that people look at marriage as a relationship of support. They put a huge burden on themselves to have a perfect relationship, and they tend to give up when they experience friction and difficulty."

Working with engaged couples, I try to take a broader view of marriage that includes the psychological elements as well as the spiritual. This approach involves having the engaged couple ask themselves, "What are you bringing to the marital bed?"

For myself, my self inventory meant admitting I came from a family with a lot of family pride (or, as my wife might say, arrogance). First, if you were in my family of the Corrs from Legaginney, much was expected of you. Second, I was the seventh of nine children, which I discovered in my adult life meant that I was continually trying to keep up or outdo those six siblings in front of me: I was and am very competitive. Third, I inherited a quick temper from my dad, which was fortunately complemented by the forgiving heart I inherited from my mom.

Surprisingly, our previous Holy Father Pope John Paul II had written some good material on marriage and sexuality. Some was written before his pontificate and some while he served as our spiritual leader. In one of his writings he stated that the Church should listen to married couples. That was an unusual comment coming from the Vatican, which was often accused of listening to nobody but themselves. He went on to describe marriage as the "total and mutual self giving of the two partners that finds its fullest expression in their sexual relationship." As you might expect, not everyone accepted the Holy Father's teaching, especially the feminists in the US, who countered that an emphasis on the complementary role of man and woman in marriage puts too much emphasis on gender differences. Sydney Callahan, a well-respected and popular writer, commented that the pope's view of marriage was "highly romantic" even though he obviously had a high regard for both marriage and women.

In my years as a licensed marriage and family therapist since August of 1973, I have come to believe that the biggest change in society to effect marriage and family life has been the change in gender roles. I came from a culture in Ireland, where men like my dad did little more than boil water when it came to cooking. If my mom hadn't cooked, I believe Dad would have starved. As you will learn later, I did not marry a traditional wife who spends half her day cooking, dusting and ironing.

About six months after my marriage to Laurie, my former secretary from St Vincent's parish in Madison NJ asked me if Laurie ironed my suit each day before I went to the office. I jokingly said, "I don't know. I will ask Laurie." When I told Laurie about the query, she replied, "That is the wrong question. She should be asking if Laurie owns an iron!?"

It is no secret that, if the average family in the US is going to keep up with the Joneses and have their own home in the suburbs with the accompanying mortgage, both parents need to work. With both parents working, new problems may arrive first for the marriage and later for the children. Major problems facing young couples are lack of time for each other, lack of sexual relations and worrying about money. With the added time and pressure of nurturing and raising children, you have to ask yourself, "Is it any wonder that the romantic feelings expected in marriage are put to a serious test?"

People in the United States, in general, have a particular disadvantage when it comes to sharing themselves totally in marriage. We are all socialized to think of ourselves first as individuals in contrast to people in the East, who are raised to think of themselves as members of a family first and individuals second. It was no surprise to many of us that when the American team competed against the Europeans in the 2002 Ryder Cup, they won most of the single matches but didn't win many of the matches that involved playing with a teammate. One sports analyst on the European side observed that the European team played as a team while the American team played as individuals. Some people would disagree with his conclusion, but the analogy to the difficulty that some Americans have in being good team members is, as far as marriage is concerned, still applicable.

Gail Risch, a researcher with Creighton Center for Marriage and Family, says that the concept of marriage as covenant is at odds with American Individualism: "Covenant is about how 'we' are doing; individualism is about how 'I' am doing." I admit that I am prejudiced to believe that what you bring to the marriage is key to how the marriage and the subsequent family will function. We weren't considered poor sixty years ago when I was a young boy in Legaginney, but by today's standard, both in Ireland and in the US, we were poor.

I feel that I was raised with a big advantage as a child, which made life easier for me in boarding school in the seminary, in the 28 years in the priesthood and lastly as a married man. The advantage was that, as one of nine children, I was taught how to share a bed, food and clothing with my siblings. It was a common practice that the older sisters passed on their dresses to younger sisters once they had outgrown them. That practice led to some funny situations.

Someone once complimented my sister Dympna on her beautiful dress and how lovely she looked in it. Dympna, without even a smile on her face, said "Thank you! It belonged to my sister Marie, Lord rest her." Marie hadn't died; she had gone into the convent to become a nun. To Dympna, who enjoyed dating and hanging out with boys, this decision of Marie's was as bad as dying.

In our family, as in many Irish families, it was expected that individuals would sacrifice for the good of the whole family. It was quite common that in a large family several children would be denied the opportunity to go to secondary school because the family finances could only afford to send one child to boarding school. That one child would most often be the one destined to make the whole family proud by becoming a priest, of course.

I am fortunate that the woman in my life, Laurie, also came from a family where the three sisters and one brother formed a deep bond of mutual support and friendship that still flourishes after 50 years. Although historically raised as part of the 'me generation' of the Fifties and Sixties, at an early age they developed (with a lot of help from a loving mother) the belief that there is more fulfillment in life if you are noncompetitive with your siblings and supportive of each other in overcoming the bumps in life.

Marriage is definitely a challenge in today's society, where every thing seems to be created for obsolescence. If you are about to marry and want to have a fulfilling life with your partner, you must first have a good understanding of what you bring as an individual to the relationship. If you have quick temper and tend to dominate people, it would help a lot if you truthfully acknowledge these negative characteristics. There is no shame in deciding to go to a therapist and learn how to make personal adjustments so as not to hurt the relationship you are entering with the one you love. If you are already married and having difficulties, then I would suggest that you look at the psychological mirror and honestly answer, "What am I contributing to the difficulties in the marriage?"

Finally, the expanded focus of marriage makes the covenant more real and acceptable to couples who embrace the challenge of marriage as a commitment of love between two human beings capable of making mistakes, of forgiving and being forgiven.

Chapter 2
I met my Husband in Church

During the years when I gave marriage and family life talks to college students, or to teenagers, I was frequently asked, "Father Corr, I don't like hanging out in bars or clubs, so I don't have much opportunity to meet somebody nice to date. What do you suggest I do?"

I would usually respond with, "Congratulations, you've asked an excellent question. Where you meet your future spouse and getting to know the company he or she keeps can be the key to knowing how that spouse is going to be as a lifetime partner."

On a personal note, whenever my wife Laurie and I are at a party or gathering where nobody is familiar with my background as a Catholic priest, someone inevitably asks her "How did you two meet? He is obviously Irish born because of that accent and you are American." She answers with a straight face, "Oh, we met in church." She never leads with, "He was the pastor of the parish, where I served on the Social Ministry Committee." This is how it actually happened.

To give newcomers an opportunity to meet each other and to learn how to become an active member in one of the forty or so parish committees, the Parish Council organized a welcoming get together every six months at the home of one of the well established parishioners. On one of these special evenings, I was walking into the host family's driveway when I bumped into an attractive young woman who was on her way to the meeting. I could only see her smiling face in the dark as she greeted me with "Good evening, Father Finbarr. I am really enjoying St. Vincent's Parish." If she told me her name, I didn't remember it. I was just thinking about why she was there alone. "Does she have a husband?" I wondered.

Our hostess, Gloria, met us both at the door and, with her usual sense of humor, said to the lady. "I see you are escorting

Father Finbarr tonight." The lady protested mildly and said "No, we just met in the driveway. When I saw him, I knew I was at the right house."

As I left her home that evening, Gloria told me, "That lady you asked about is Laurie Hutton. She is single, never married, a native of Kansas and lives in Convent Station. I noticed that you two were looking at each other a lot tonight, Father Finbarr, so you'd better watch out," she added with a smile.

When I started to date Laurie a year later, after I had decided to leave the priesthood, I began to realize that I was fulfilling many of the goals and objectives I had spoken about or preached about for years. Helping people to recognize the importance of where they met their fiancé, what company their romantic partner kept and of what were the cultural, educational and religious compatibilities or differences between them was part the initial inventory I sought from the engaged couple.

Laurie had a big advantage over me in that she had known me as a public figure for several years before we became emotionally involved. She had learned a lot about me from my homilies on Sunday mornings and from my ongoing interaction with people in the parish. She knew very well that I was a flaming extrovert who enjoyed being with people and, more than all of that, enjoyed making new people who joined our parish family of St Vincent's feel very welcome. Her phase of "getting to know you" got a head start over my seeing her as "just another smiling face" in church phase.

There was an age difference between us, but not enough to make it an insurmountable obstacle to growth as a couple. We both knew that I was very young at heart and was quite capable of keeping up with a younger woman as a life partner. Later on, when we became serious about our relationship and were planning on getting married, my therapist raised the question of how Laurie would handle relating to a husband who, for several years, had enjoyed being put on a pedestal by his parishioners. She answered him very forthrightly, "Dr. Gerson, I am not planning on replacing the 1,800 families that he meets every Sunday morning."

Since I am trying to be honest here in helping other couples develop an open and loving relationship, I must admit that in the years since we married unrealistic expectations have been more of a problem for me than for Laurie. Having had my personal needs met by secretaries, housekeepers and lay volunteers over 28 years, I do have an unconscious expectation that Laurie will drop whatever she is doing to address my immediate need. This confession on my part will hopefully serve as a message to prospective grooms who have been spoiled by their mothers. Don't expect your future wife to wait on you hand and foot just like your mama did for twenty or thirty years.

Counseling couples who came from different cultures gave me insight into how difficult it can be for each party to understand the behavior and communication from their spouse. The most dramatic case I experienced was a couple where the husband was an all-American white professional man who taught at a community college. His wife was a very attractive educated woman born in the Brahmin caste in India. She was raised according to her culture to believe that professional men do not do manual work. While they got along brilliantly on issues like sexual relations, parenting and entertaining each other's relatives, she had serious problems with his doing manual work over the summer months.

Initially she didn't know how to let him know that she was very embarrassed to have to tell her Indian girlfriends that she and her husband couldn't accept Saturday invitations because her husband had taken on a six-day-a-week job installing swimming pools during the summer. When he came home sweaty and dirty from work, rather than sharing her feelings, she would give him the silent treatment and withhold sex from him for the weekend. In spite of his educational background, he hadn't the faintest idea what he had done to offend her. When he asked her what was wrong, he only got silence.

Having a quick temper, he blurted out, "You stupid bitch! I don't know what you want from me. I go and get a second job to increase our income and all I get is silence." That only added more fuel to the fire because professional men in the Brahmin caste don't use vulgar language.

Another very common cultural difference I came across was counseling a couple where one party was of Italian or Spanish background and the other was white Anglo-Saxon Protestant. Angelo was an architect born in Italy and had been successfully employed for several years in New Jersey before he married Jane, an only daughter of a wealthy Presbyterian American couple. While she appreciated his warmth and caring personality, she had serious problems with the wide boundaries of his tendency to share family information. When they had been married about ten years, Antonio was surprised one Tuesday morning when his boss called him into his office one morning and said, "Antonio, I have been very satisfied with your work over the past few years, I think it is time we extended your responsibilities in the company. How would like managing the new project we just acquired of designing the new bridge in a suburb of Chicago?"

Antonio was elated, actually ready to jump out of his skin at his boss's trust in him. Trying to keep his cool, he calmly said, "Thank you, Sir," then asked, "Is this going to involve some travel and will there be an increase in salary to go along with the new responsibility?" His boss answered with a big smile, "Antonio, the answer to both questions is yes. How does an increase of $10,000 to your annual salary sound?"

For once in his life, Antonio was speechless. Sitting back in his own office a few minutes later, he was pinching himself trying to accept this new windfall of luck. He grabbed the phone on his desk to call Jane to share the news of their good fortune. In his excitement he forgot it was Tuesday morning and that Jane always had a tennis date with a friend at that time. Because of his high emotional response, which is cultural, he couldn't wait until Jane came home from her tennis game. He remembered that his mama was always home, usually cooking pasta or some Italian delicacy for his dad's midday dinner. She was, of course, proud and very happy to hear of her son's great success in their adopted country. Mama, in turn, shared the good news with her daughter, who lived in the apartment above her. In the meantime Antonio relaxed and started working on the Chicago project and making plans to visit the site the following week. He forgot to call Jane later in the day.

As he drove home he thought, "I cannot wait to see the look on Jane's face when I tell her of our good fortune!" Bouncing in the door, he blurted out, "Jane, you better sit down while I tell you happened to me in my boss's office this morning!"

Jane didn't sit. She just stood before him as if she was a cold statue. With her arms folded over her chest, she growled, "I know. Your sister called me an hour ago" and didn't talk to him again until Friday. You see, Antonio had broken a cardinal rule that Jane's culture observed strictly. That is, you don't share any important family news, good or bad, with anybody until you first share it with your spouse.

When I was pastor in St Vincent's, at least one quarter of the marriages I witnessed involved interfaith couples and 50% were intercultural. For the interfaith couples, I had to obtain a dispensation from the Bishop's Office, and the non-Catholic partner had to agree to raise their offspring in the Catholic faith. This usually created a very serious problem if the non-Catholic happened to be Jewish. The more common practice for a marriage between a Catholic and Jew was to obtain permission from the bishop or his delegate to hold the wedding ceremony outside the church at the reception hall and have a rabbi and priest witness the marriage as a team.

One of the humorous things that happened at one of those ceremonies was receiving an invitation from the rabbi to join him as a team performing such interfaith marriages. He said. "Finbarr, I feel very comfortable working with you. We could make a lot of money also as I would split the fee with you."

I declined the offer but discovered later that he was one of the very few rabbis who witnessed marriages of Jews to Christians. He charged $450 to perform the ceremony while I, the Catholic priest, received a $25 donation. Maybe I should have thought about his generous offer a bit longer.

One of the joys as a pre-marriage counselor was to tell those young couples with cultural differences that their marriage was not destined for failure just because they were marrying somebody from a different culture. All that each needed to do was to learn and accept the values and customs of their partner. By doing that, not only would their marriage survive, but their marriage and family life would be enriched because of what each brought to the relationship. I would encourage each of the parties to discuss family customs and traditions and to frequently ask their partner, "Do you think I am doing anything or saying things that are offensive to your family?"

Open communication and sharing is the key to resolving any obstacles in marriage. Later on, when we discuss conflict resolution, I will offer some suggestions on how to decide before the wedding on issues like the religion of the children and parenting approaches.

This chapter would not be complete without raising the question of what happens when a couple has different racial or religious backgrounds that are visibly uncomfortable for the families from the beginning. If the situation is not handled correctly from the beginning, the marriage can have major problems and end up a total disaster.

When I was growing up in Ireland, it was practically unheard of for an Irish Catholic to marry a Protestant. I believe that the issue at that time in America was the fear of interracial marriage between a black person and a white person. The same anxious feelings were expressed in the popular American movie *Guess Who's Coming to Dinner* when the daughter of Katherine Hepburn and Spencer Tracey announced that her date for dinner was black and that she intended to marry him.

I recall a story from my boarding school in Ireland that we thought was hysterically funny, but was not judged politically correct by the priest faculty. It was the story of a young Irish woman who went to work in London to make some money to support her mom and siblings. She came home after a few months to celebrate Christmas with her family sporting a beautiful long mink coat. Her family was in total shock as to how she could make some much to buy a mink coat and save enough for her boat fare back to Ireland in just a few months. Her mom, of course, asked her about her sudden financial windfall. She replied with certain arrogance, "Mom, I am a prostitute." Her mother almost fainted and blurted back, "What did you say?" Her daughter answered more timidly this time. "Mom, I am a prostitute." Her Mom responded, "Oh, thank God! I thought you said you said you were a Protestant."

Although I had had extensive experience with interfaith marriages, including the experience of being the first Catholic priest in New Jersey to witness an interfaith marriage in a Protestant church, I have had very limited experience of interracial marriages. One of the first questions I always raised with engaged couples of different races, was "How are each of your families accepting your decision?"

If either of them said that their family was totally against it, I offered to meet with those parents or siblings to help them move from intolerance to acceptance and support. Being as sensitive and nonjudgmental as possible, I would ask the couple if they planned to have children. If the answer was yes (as it usually was), I would ask them how they planned to help their children deal with the prejudice that their children might suffer from both black children and white children.

I am happy to report that the few interracial marriages I witnessed turned out very well and the couples were very appreciative of the sensitivity with which I handled the situation. If an interracial couple have any doubts, before they marry they should reach out to a competent pre-marriage counselor and have sessions to resolve any possible issues.

Cultural differences can have a profound effect on a marital relationship and place demands on both parties not just to understand and accept what they personally bring from their culture to the marital bed, but also to learn and accept the culture of their spouse.

Chapter 3
Getting to Know You

As I reported earlier, Laurie knew me a lot better than I knew her. She had observed the way I treated women in various ministries as pastor and saw that I was comfortable in dealing with women. If she had met me 20 years earlier, she probably wouldn't have found me attractive. By the time we met, I had grown from telling women what to do in ministries to discussing with them various options in carrying out their tasks as a prelude to their making the decision.

As a parishioner, she did not directly experience the negative aspects of my personality like my quick Irish temper and my unconscious desire to be always number one. What she did experience was a pastor who was very highly respected and loved by his parishioners, for the basic reason that he had matured and had the training necessary, to nurture a loving and caring parish.

In my quest to get to know Laurie better I got a break when on one of Sunday morning she introduced me to two elegant ladies. "Father Finbarr, I'd like to introduce my mother Mary and my sister Michele from Kansas. This is their first visit to New Jersey and I wanted them to meet you and experience the liturgy at St Vincent's."

I invited them to come over with Laurie for coffee at the rectory. Mary initiated the conversation, saying, "My family is of Irish descent. My grandmother was a Neary from County Wexford, and I have a very warm spot in my heart for the Irish. Years ago in our little town of Holyrood we had a wonderful Irish priest by the name of Father Kenny. Your humor from the pulpit this morning reminded me a lot of him. He would frequently come to our home after Sunday mass and have breakfast before he went on to visit other parishes. The last we heard of him was that he returned to Ireland, married and had several children."

I tried to see the reaction in Laurie's face but she turned to her sister and changed the conversation. Before I escorted the three ladies to the door, Mary added, "We miss Laurie very much, but we but we are happy to see that she has found a friendly parish that has become her spiritual home."

Now I was certain that not only did Laurie like priests, but her whole family enjoyed having a priest as part of their family. Little did anyone know that within a year Laurie's mother was going to have an Irish priest as a son-in-law. I gave Mary and Michele a warm embrace goodbye and said, "Maybe next time you will bring Mr. Hutton along."

All three of them laughed. Laurie said, "Daddy is a home body. He says he did enough traveling during the war when he served in the US Air Force."

I shook Laurie's hand goodbye. To be honest, I wanted to give her a big hug, but I wasn't ready to let her know what strong feelings I had for her. After they left, I remember saying to myself, "Laurie and I have a lot in common. We are both Catholic, she is at least 25% Irish, she loves her family and they adore her."

I was beginning to feel that my prayers were being answered, having already made up my mind that I wanted to get married to someone of the same religion and similar cultural background (i.e., Irish). I had taught young people over the years that it is easier to make a marriage work if the two parties have similar backgrounds. I knew then that, if disagreements were to develop between Laurie and me, we would have fewer psychological barriers to overcome.

In my pre-marriage counseling over the years, I had focused on helping young people understand that it was very important to learn as much as possible about their future spouse during the courtship phase of their relationship. Because the courtship period is not very natural since both party is putting on their best face to impress their date, Laurie and I looked for time and stress-free opportunities to get to know the real person that the other was.

We both agreed that there was definitely a strong emotional and romantic attraction to each other, which is the first and necessary ingredient of a lifelong relationship. Laurie was very open in sharing her personal history of previous relationships she had. I also shared of how I had struggled with celibacy over the last 13 years and how I had at times being unfaithful to my vows as a priest. I also shared that it would be difficult for me to leave the priesthood, as I had many deep relationships with fellow priests, and that my decision to resign would be a big disappointment to my family and the thousands of lay people who held me in high esteem as "Father Finbarr."

I share this part of my personal story here to let you, the reader, know that, first of all, openness and honesty are very important during the engagement period as well as when you are married. Secondly, there may be attachments in your life that you have to let go of to avoid distractions from growth in your marriage.

We both shared the history of our families so that there would not be any surprises down the road. Laurie's family was always very close and more communicative. The Corr clan, living all over Ireland, London and America were, for obvious reasons, not in contact on a day-to-day basis. The competitiveness among the Corr siblings seem to be absent from Laurie's family. We were both accustomed to strong father figures, with my dad being more the silent one, who left most of the disciplining to my mom. Laurie's dad was more vocal and accustomed to giving directions. He still acted as if he was still a police officer. We each had a warm, affectionate and religious mom who had strongly influenced our personality.

The same basic religious training we both received by word and example from our moms (and dads too) was to become one of the strengths of our marriage. Once we chose a parish, we not only attended mass regularly but volunteered as a couple to assist the parish in conducting Pre-Cana sessions for engaged couples in our home. In contrast to our experience, while I was dating Laurie I interviewed a former priest who had resigned after 19 years in active ministry to then become a very successful entrepreneur on Wall Street. He married a woman of the Jewish faith, and they then had a son circumcised and raised in the Jewish faith. He said he no longer attended the Catholic Church. I wondered what my married priest friend did for a support system if he gave up his religion and the support of all his priest friends. Marrying someone who is spiritually as well as socially and emotionally compatible can make your marriage a much easier journey - and more fun besides.

An old saying in Ireland was "He will be the same person after you marry him as he was before, only worse." This was particularly true of a young lady in our town in Ireland who dated a known alcoholic. She was highly respected by the whole community, and several of her close friends advised her against marrying him. She did not heed their advice. Three months after she married him, coming home from town after having too many pints of Guinness, he crashed his truck and did himself and his truck serious damage.

When asked by one of the distinguished women in town as to why she married him, she simply replied, "Probably, because so many people were forcing me not to marry him." He had promised her on his oath that he would slow down on the boozing after they were married and stop altogether within a year. None of these promises were kept.

The same philosophy and scrutiny could be applied to any unacceptable characteristics that you discover in your intended spouse. If you discover that he or she is very intolerant of any minority and this is very offensive to you, you should know that marriage is not going to convert him or her. He is not going to be suddenly tolerant of all the various people who are going to be your neighbors for the next 40 or 50 years. The same insight applies to drug addicts, gamblers, and men who spend a lot of time viewing pornography on the internet. Marriage is not going to cure their addiction.

On the other hand, there may be things that you do decide to live with. You don't always have to have the same political views as your spouse. I know several couples where the husband is a diehard Republican and the wife is a Democrat. They are able to joke about it and laugh when I tell them, that it is okay if they both skip the national elections, as their votes cancel out one another anyway.

In my own marriage I quickly realized that my being an extrovert always ready to share a story or take over a party, while entertaining for the guests, is not necessarily entertaining for my wife. Once on our way home from what I commented was a very enjoyable evening with neighbors, she replied honestly, "I know you enjoyed yourself, as you dominated the conversation the whole evening."

I had no defense, so I simply said, "I am sorry, Honey, you are right. I don't know why that happens."

She very kindly responded, "I know why and will tell you if you want to hear it."

"Go ahead, I am a big boy and can handle it."

She continued, "As a priest you were used to being the center of attention, and you are a funny person, but it is not enjoyable for me if your personality shuts me out of most conversations at a party."

This story is my confession that getting married didn't make me an introvert. I did however learn to make an adjustment and now will frequently stop before telling a story to say, "Laurie why don't you tell them what happened to us last week on our recent trip."

As we will discuss later, good honest feedback given nonjudgementally does not have to be a negative experience in the marriage. Once a decision is made to commit to each other, a spouse has a responsibility to allow their partner to be himself or herself, or otherwise they are both wasting a lot of time and energy pretending to be someone they are not.

With commitment, tolerance should also follow. One of the nicest characteristics that my spouse has is that she doesn't hold grudges or carry on a fight for days as some spouses do. I guess she realizes that we are both human and living in close community with each other, and that we are going to make mistakes and offend each other unintentionally. Marriage is a series of "I am sorry, Honey, I didn't mean to hurt you" and the response "I accept your apology, and I didn't think you would deliberately do so and so to hurt me."

A healthy marriage also involves being sensitive to the physical needs of your spouse. Sometimes that involves agreeing to go on a diet in support of a spouse who has trouble controlling their weight. Encouraging them to play golf with you, joining a gym, or going for a vigorous half hour walk with your wife or husband can be a very loving act. Offering to take in the groceries from the trunk of her car can be a way of saying thank you for doing the food shopping. Women usually have more tolerance for work at home that needs patience and endurance, but expecting them to cut the grass on a Saturday afternoon while you watch college football can hardly be interpreted as a division of labor in the home.

The bottom line is that growth in marriage and preparing for a life-giving and creative relationship involves some careful planning, open and honest communication, and commitment to grow in understanding and appreciation of the other. Putting it bluntly, you get back from the relationship what you put into it.

I advocate that engaged and newly married couples have what I call a "one-on-one" discussion every three months about the marital relationship. Each party should be free from all distraction like watching TV or expecting a phone call. Laurie and I often use the time made available when we are on long rides together to visit family in Kansas or Ireland. Either party can begin by stating what they like about the marriage and then list the things that they would like changed. The other party listens nonjudgementally and nondefensively, and then shares similar feelings about what they like or would like to see changed.   Laurie and I have used this system for years to great advantage in building a loving and fun relationship. In this simple manner, we get rid of those little negative feelings that will inevitably creep into any marital relationship, no matter how strong.

Chapter 4
Searching for Intimacy

As part of our getting to know each other early in our relationship, Laurie and I followed through on our plan to take time off and spend time together without any distractions from our job responsibilities. Laurie fixed a nice picnic basket and we headed for the hills of Pennsylvania. Our conversation flowed very easily, and we were both relaxed and open with each other. She shared that she had broken a past engagement. She already had come to the resolution that marriage was not going to be part of her life's plan.

At one point, she looked at me with those big knowing eyes and asked, "Have you ever thought of marriage yourself?" She continued after a slight pause, "I can tell by your homilies over the past few years and observing you flirting with women in the parish that you would prefer to be married, if you had that option."

Her openness and direct questioning threw me back a little but I decided that this was not a time to be coy or play with her feelings. I admitted, "The real reason I took half a year off from the parish last year was to discern if I wanted to be celibate over the next 25 years. I discovered after months of prayer and consultation with spiritual directors both in California and Rome, that I didn't have what we call the charism of celibacy."

I went on with some emotion to say, "I guess you have known for awhile that I find you very attractive." She nodded back and said, "I recognized that."

As I had counseled other couples over the years, we began to share our personal and family histories, as we wandered along the paths or just sat on the sunny side of a mountain. It felt very strange for me at the outset, as I was usually the one sitting listening to my engaged clients sharing with me how they met, what their families had in common, or roadblocks they were experiencing along the road to marital intimacy.

Over the years I developed skills at leading both parties to let go of their personal defenses and to be open in sharing their family history in the sessions. Now I felt drawn to the same goals and challenge for this new and special person in my life. It was obvious that Laurie and I possessed the same strong family values. We were both raised to believe that belief in God and the power of personal prayer would carry us through most challenges in life. Laurie's Dad was a convert to Catholicism and enjoyed all of the old traditional devotions and rituals that were part of the church services for centuries until the Second Vatican Council. As the day progressed, it became clearer to me and to Laurie also, that this was not just a nice day in the country.

My concern at the end of that beautiful and enjoyable day was not whether Laurie Hutton's family and the Corrs of Legaginney were going to be compatible. I was more concerned about how I was going to get to know and appreciate her as she really was, and would she risk and tolerate marriage to a man who for years had allowed people to put him on a pedestal. I was accustomed to having my own way and freedom to do as I wanted in social situations. I knew that if I married Laurie or any woman for that matter, I would have to sacrifice this free-wheeling egotistical way of living and participate in a 50-50 decision making relationship for the rest of my life.

I was already conscious that Laurie's dad was a strong character from stories her mom and sister Michele had shared with me over coffee at the rectory. Laurie had probably learned over the years how to stand up to strong male figures and would not be intimidated by either my tendency to dominate or my tendency to manipulate people with a load of Irish blarney. If the relationship was going to make progress, I would have to raise these sensitive questions with Laurie and at the same time warn her that along with the charm of an Irish brogue, I was bringing the baggage of a quick Irish temper.

As we finished our first "official" date, we each resolved to pray individually about our relationship. During future visits, we would pray together for guidance. Laurie even volunteered to compose a small prayer that we would recite together. While reflecting on all of this, I found myself thanking God for our good fortune in finding each other. While other couples our age were searching through unfamiliar channels to meet others, we had literally found each other in Church.

Looking back now I wonder if I used all the criteria that I had preached over the years to young people about the selection of a marital partner and which of the theories I had exercised in deciding that Laurie Hutton was the one. Sociologies Ira Reiss wrote in 1960 about what is commonly called "the opposites attract" theory. He claimed that individuals are attracted to those whose needs closely match their own. Thus a dominant person and submissive person would tend to be attracted to each other. I don't believe that theory applied to Laurie and me, as we were both strong people. Any need that Laurie may have had to be submissive to strong men was resolved years before she met Finbarr Corr.

Our goals then included learning how to compromise, which is an integral part of any marital relationship. If either Laurie or I had married in our twenties, when couples usually marry, I expect that she would have been attracted to a strong person in any case, while I would have been attracted to someone who either wanted to mother me or to a woman who looked up to me as a leader. As it turned out, we both married an equal.

Over the years as I met with and helped couples prepare for marriage, I asked them to share with me and with each other what hobbies and interests they had in common. Couples who enjoy the same sport activities and have similar cultural interests will obviously spend more time together. Over the years Laurie and I have found that sharing such activities, rather than leading to our getting on each other's nerves, as some people expect, has helped us enjoy each other's company at a deeper level. When we were younger, we enjoyed dancing, and looked for any opportunity to do so. Because Laurie always enjoys a good movie, I willingly accompany her and subsequently discuss what we each got out of the movie.

Like me, Laurie was an athlete in high school and college, playing basketball, running track, and playing tennis. She surprised me by telling me she was good at golf, having learned to play golf with her grandfather back in Kansas while still in grade school. When I told her I was an avid golfer, she gave me a big smile and offered, "I will play golf with you even though I don't find playing the game as fulfilling as you do." Eighteen years later, I am very happy to report we play golf together twice a week.

Our hobbies and sport activities were not determined by our personal preferences only. We were frequently influenced by what else was available in the community where we lived. When we moved to beautiful Cape Cod, we found ourselves attracted to taking long walks on the beach and kayaking on many of the area's waterways.

While we enjoy our time recreating together, we also respect the time that each of needs to do things separately. I enjoy the times that I can withdraw to my "cave" and spend time writing, planting and taking care of our flowers, bushes and trees. Laurie enjoys reading political and business books and helping her family with projects. I spend some solo time doing volunteer work with Rotary International, and Laurie sometimes joins me in many of their social and fundraising activities.

Over the years I have encouraged and witnessed many couples doing volunteer work together either at their church, synagogue or fraternal organization. I have great admiration for one couple from New Jersey with deep philanthropic values who organizes trips for themselves and other folks to go into New York City weekly to take food to the homeless. In their counseling sessions they have told me how their ministry has enriched their marriage and helped them appreciate their own good fortune of having more than their share of this world's goods.

Over the years, as a director of a diocesan agency and as a pastor, I have witnessed firsthand the emotional growth of couples who volunteered to counsel engaged couples or worked together in social ministry to the sick or the poor. I hope that the reader, whether newly engaged or now married several years, can appreciate the unlimited value of discerning and seeking to know and understand their partner on many levels – intellectual, emotional and spiritual – and know that it is time well spent.

Chapter 5
Marriage as a Family Outing

My mother-in-law, Mary Frances, is a very devout Catholic, who was married to Kenneth, a convert to Catholicism. She prayed that all of her four children would marry Catholics. As luck would have it, her oldest daughter married a Quaker, the next daughter married a Lutheran and her son married a Methodist.

When it was Laurie's turn to get married, her sister Michele said to Mary Frances, "Mom, don't you think that you overdid it in praying that Laurie marry a Catholic, now that she is marrying a priest?"

When I told the story to my bishop a few years later, even he thought it was funny. Being hooked up with another family through marriage is not necessarily funny. The in-laws, whether they are the parents of your spouse or siblings, can contribute a lot to the happiness of a marriage or to its demise. As I have commented earlier, your marriage has a better chance of survival and growth if both parties have similar ethnic, cultural and religious backgrounds.

Most marriage and family therapists would agree that there is a positive correlation between the background variables of the couples and fulfillment in marriage. This is particularly true when the bride and groom are the same age, have similar educational backgrounds, and enjoy the same hobbies and recreational activities. If you feel totally accepted by your in-laws and you are equally comfortable with them, you should thank God for this blessing.

I wish I could say that all of my engaged clients over the years were as lucky as I have been. Many people were so anxious to get married that they did not take a hard look at the family of their prospective spouse. One young man left his homeland in Europe and came over to take advantage of the American dream. He worked hard as a carpenter and truck driver, saved his money, and bought his own apartment. While he enjoyed life in the new world, with all of the excitement of dancing with his colleagues and flirting with women at the local nightclubs, he did not have any plan to date an American woman with the intention of marriage. His goals were to save a few thousand dollars, go back to Poland, buy his own farm, and marry a local Polish woman.

He was shocked to see that the American girls were not shy and inhibited like the girls back home in Poland. Because he was tall and handsome, the American girls found him very attractive. He bought them their favorite cocktails, as he was accustomed to do at home, and which the local American boys did not do. In fact, several girls of Polish extraction were vying for his attention.

In the meantime, Stephen was enjoying all the attention. He had not been that popular with the young women in his native village. In fact, very few women liked him because he had a reputation as a lazy smart aleck, whose goal in dating was to take sexual liberties with naïve girls in the village. In the next few months, a group of women followed him to different nightclubs. One of the women finally invited him to come visit her family in a little town about 20 miles away. The young woman's family became excited, as they were concerned that their daughter, now in her early thirties, was unable to retain boyfriends. They were doubly appreciative because her new beau Stephen was Polish like them.

Marie and Stephen dated for about six months and, since Stephen did not have any immediate family in the US, they spent a lot of their courtship visiting her family and enjoying Marie's moms cooking. What Stephen did not realize was that Marie's family was hardworking, and their apparent wealth was the result of years of attention to their goal of building the best houses in their town. He did not realize that if he married their daughter and joined the family business, he would be working hard ten hours a day. His focus during their courtship was on having his sexual needs fulfilled.

For her part, Marie was afraid of losing him as had happened several times before with other boyfriends. She agreed to sexual intimacies. She did not want to get pregnant, so she insisted that Stephen use contraceptives. Marie couldn't have known that Stephen was very lazy or that his laidback attitude towards work was no match for her dad's or her two brothers' work ethic. He always had plenty of spending money and gave her nice gifts at the holidays. In simple terms, neither party was aware of who they were falling in love with. Since Stephen came from a rather poor family in Poland, he was looking at the relationship and a possible future with Marie through rose-colored glasses. To add to the myth, Marie's dad offered to build a new home for her.

One Christmas, Stephen proposed marriage and followed the traditional Polish custom of first approaching her dad for her hand in marriage. He should have first asked himself, "Am I ready to take on this hardworking, motivated family?"

Marie could have done a little more research with Stephen's colleagues to better assess his compatibility with her very close-knit family. Because she did not want to appear a failure before her family or her community, she ignored some tendencies he had to control her and be critical of her eating habits. She did not follow her intuitions and delay her decision but instead said, "Yes, Stephen, I will marry you and have your children."

Three months into the marriage, Stephen made his second mistake. His new father-in-law offered him a position with his company. Stephen accepted it and, by doing that, gave up any independence from his in-laws that he would need later in the marriage. Within two months, Stephen realized that he could not keep up with these workaholic in-laws. Not only did they work ten hours a day Monday through Friday, but they would also sometimes want Stephen to work on Saturdays and Sundays without any extra compensation for overtime. He naturally complained to his wife, which Marie interpreted as being ungrateful to her father, whom she had adored her whole life.

Within the first year of the marriage, a baby girl arrived; a boy followed twelve months later. Since Stephen was not getting any support from Marie regarding his dissatisfaction working for her dad, he quit the company and went back to his old job.

After just three years, there was no relationship between Stephen and his in-laws. Marie took her parents' side. His parents, sensing some serious trouble, made a visit from Poland. Marie was gracious and made them feel very welcome. However, she made the mistake of saying to them, "Your son is lazy and cannot match my dad and my brothers."

That was the straw that broke the camel's back. After Stephen heard about his wife's complaint to his parents, he was very hurt. He attacked her verbally and said, "You are nothing but a self-centered bitch. You simply used me to have children, and now you are prepared to dump me as you don't need my money or my love." Stephen didn't realize early enough that marrying Marie was marrying her whole family.

I have also witnessed similar situations where a prospective American groom went to Europe to meet a prospective bride. In one situation, the bride's family was very impressed with the American's riches. Both the bride and her family overlooked the fact that he was much older than she was, and much more conservative than she and her family. She was also very much attached and overly dependent on her sisters. In spite of all that, the couple married in Italy and moved to the United States right away. Working hard at his profession, the husband needed to spend several days at a time away from his beautiful wife. Unable to drive a car and slow to make friends, the wife felt like a prisoner in their home.

To compensate for her loneliness she made frequent phone calls to her parents and sisters back home, thus never becoming independent from her family of origin. Her patient husband Anthony did not fuss about the big phone bills or her requests to visit her family every other year. One winter she got so depressed that she asked Anthony to drive her to the airport for yet another trip home. This time she had two extra bags of clothes, which caused him some concern. When he asked her why she was carrying so many suitcases, she replied, "My dad is very sick, so I might stay an extra month in case he takes a turn for the worse and dies."

While in Italy, she grew very depressed at the thought of leaving her family again. She stayed two years. Her family did not encourage her to go back and join her husband. It was at this time that Anthony realized that he not only married a beautiful woman but also that he was hooked to a whole family who were controlling his marriage from thousands of miles away.

As I mentioned earlier, some cultures in the East do not have the same courtship and selection processes for marriage as we have in the West. In India the choice of marital partner is sometimes made by the parents of the bride and groom. Their primary concern is to match couples from the same caste system and avoid cultural conflicts as much as possible. In this way, the bride or groom's decision to accept the recommendation of the parents includes accepting the other's family as well. In the beginning, both the bride and groom are emotionally and physically dependent on their families. The young couple actually lives in the home of their in-laws.

I have counseled couples from India who told me horror stories of how their mother-in-laws demanded more of the new bride than of their own daughters. If the demands became extreme, the new brides could always appeal to their own parents for support. The question that remains unresolved is whether our Western system of choosing a partner based on sexual attraction and passion is more prone to failure than leaving it to the parents or tribal leaders to choose a spouse. One thing is clearer for certain: in the Eastern culture, when you say "Yes" on your wedding day and make your marital vows, you know you are taking on a family as well as an individual spouse.

Getting married in a Western culture can be catastrophic especially when both families think they know each other's families very well. Unfortunately, both parties' visions of what the marriage will be like can be clouded by a psychological need to be married. There is a certain type of woman who does not feel complete unless she is married, just as there men who are so dependent on their mothers that if one wife leaves them by death or divorce, they need to quickly marry again to survive.

When these two types meet and get involved, it is very difficult to get them to understand that there is a lot more to marriage than just fulfilling psychological needs. In one particular case the husband was so anxious to be married that he called his beloved daily. He lied about his age and wealth saying that he owned villas in Europe. He kept pressing until she said yes. I offered to counsel the bride-to-be, but she was not open to listening to logic or slowing down her decision. She told me I did not understand the situation and that her family had known him for years.

I had only been counseling engaged couples for close to forty years at that point and was not convinced that she was making the right decision. Margaret gave a very positive, glowing report about the wedding, telling me the ceremony was beautiful, and the honeymoon mostly enjoyable. Then she paused and admitted she was not happy to discover on the honeymoon that her husband had lied about his age. He was actually eighteen years older than she was, not twelve as he had told her before the wedding. I asked her how the stepchildren accepted her. She went silent for a moment and said, "I have to be honest with you. I believe they all resent me taking the place of their dead mother."

Trying to be very empathic, I replied, "I am really sorry, Margaret, that they don't recognize what a good person you are, and how you will make their dad a very happy man. Didn't his daughter help you plan the wedding?"

She reacted instantly. "Are you kidding? We were lucky that she came to the wedding."

As the marriage progressed, Margaret felt very unaccepted by her stepchildren. The new husband did not empathize with her feeling of being rejected and would go off alone to visit his children. The bottom line is that Margaret did not realize what she was getting into and certainly did not understand that when you marry a husband you are also marrying his children.

If you possess similar values and attitudes as the family you are now married to, life will be much easier and enjoyable for all concerned. If there are areas where you, the bride or groom, have a different political orientation than your father- or mother-in-law, my recommendation is that you keep away from discussing politics.

In my particular situation, my father in-law, who is now deceased, enjoyed teasing me about my affection for the Kennedy clan in Massachusetts. Because he was an admitted Republican, I deliberately avoided getting into a serious discussion about politics for the 15 years he lived after my marriage to his daughter Laurie. For fun, whenever I wanted to get a rise out of him, I would say upon arrival at his home, "Before I forget it … Hillary said to say hello to you." The reference was to Mrs. Clinton, who was at that time a US senator from New York. I don't want to print his reply here, but he knew that I was teasing him.

My mother-in-law, a very spiritual woman, enjoys discussing religion and psychological issues with me. Laurie's living siblings have become best friends. They are a very close-knit family, which I totally respect.

For Laurie, marrying me meant not only accepting all the Corr clan from Legaginney but also getting to know and accept the larger family of fellow priests and friends that I had developed over the 28 years in the ministry. If I can be so presumptuous as to give her a grade for being up to the challenge, I feel she has earned an A +.

Chapter 6
Making the Commitment

Marriage counselors like me tell many stories of men who fall in love, promise their girlfriends the world, and then don't follow through and get married. Conversely, women as a rule are more prepared to make a commitment and get married as soon as they have decided "He is the one for me." In my professional experience I found that most young women, while rejoicing over getting a proposal for marriage, were not satisfied until he said "I do" at the altar and they walked back down the aisle together as husband and wife.

Common law marriages were very popular in the early days of the United States when couples settled in sparsely populated areas where priests and ministers were not readily available. Sometimes after several years and some children, a priest or minister in church might validate the marriage. According to sociologist and author Robert Francoeur, one in five cohabiting American couples was not legally married in the 1920s. Until 1968, 15 states accepted common law marriages as legitimate to protect the family and legitimize the children.

When I was growing up in Ireland, a common law marriage was unheard off. If a local young fellow was known to be dating the same woman for years with no commitment yet to marry and if there was a suspicion of physical intimacy between them, the fellows hanging out at the local crossroads would say, "Why should he buy the cow when he can get the milk for nothing?"

Just as the practice of couples living together before marriage is increasing again in the US, it is also increasing in England and even in "Holy" Ireland. Even if I was tempted to enter such a relationship with Laurie, this option was never a possibility. Laurie said on one of our very first times together, "I have no intention of becoming a priest's girlfriend."

When you ask a single fellow who has been dating the same woman for a long time, "Why don't you two get married, you actually do everything a married couple does?" you get a variety of answers. The most common answer is, "I like things just as they are. So many women change after marriage, and I don't want to upset the apple cart."

We used to tell a story of couple in Ireland named Pat and Bridget, who had been dating for 13 years. To give Pat a nudge towards the altar, Bridget said to him one evening on their weekly date, "Pat, the neighbors are saying we are going to be getting married!!"

Pat hesitated before he answered and said slowly, "Is that right, Bridget? Now who would want to marry either of us?"

I once had a client who was dating two women simultaneously. Almost in hysterics, he came to my office two weeks before Christmas. During the inventory phase of the first session I asked him, "Mike tell me honestly how far both of these relationships have developed?" I almost fell of my own couch when he admitted, "Dr. Corr, both of these ladies are expecting me to give them an engagement ring during the holidays!"

Continuing the inventory, I discovered that Mike had a very dominating mother who seldom allowed him to make any personal decisions without her input and approval. Both of his girl friends were also dominating. As you can guess, neither of the women received a ring for Christmas. In the next few weeks, I was able to lead Mike to understand that he needed to spend some time learning how to separate emotionally from a controlling mother. Otherwise, as we would say, his marrying one of those women, at that time, would be "jumping from the frying pan into the fire."

For other men, like me, getting married requires changing a life style and letting go of behaviors or connections that are not compatible with being married. Laurie knew that I really enjoyed being a priest and she had great empathy with the struggle I was going through. I knew that I would not get the support of some of my family and that many lay people would be very disappointed with my decision.

I was very fortunate that I had a supportive spiritual director. I also made an appointment with a very competent and caring psychologist. When I told the psychologist, Mike Gerson, that I had been very happy as a priest for over 27 years, but that I just wanted to get married, which meant having to change careers also. He just didn't say, "Fine, Finbarr, go ahead. I think that is great, good luck!" Over a couple of weeks he led me to accept that I would not be happy by just getting married, and that I needed a "ministry" to replace the priesthood in order to be happy as a married man. That is when I decided to open my own marriage and family counseling practice, with which I was very happily engaged for the next 15 years.

I have met many men and women in my counseling practice, who had fallen in love but who, because of commitments to their careers, had great difficulty making the decision to get married. To add to the dilemma, society was no longer saying to women, "You are not a complete person unless you are married." For some women, the question was "will my future husband expect me to give up my career or put my career on hold if we decide we are going to have children." The reality for most is that, if a couple marry and want to have their own home, both partners will probably have to continue some form of work outside the home to pay the mortgage.

One couple I know have worked out their commitment in such a way that the husband is the "stay-at-home" parent in charge of the home, cooking and parenting, while his wife works very hard at a demanding job to support the family. They are in the fortunate position that the wife's salary is sufficient for their needs. Other couples, needing both salaries, follow the more common approach and engage a day care center to take care of their child or children while they both work.

Recently while teaching psychology to a class that included a married man and a married woman. Both couples reported being uncomfortable using day care for their children. They decided to live with the challenge of making ends meet, within the constraints of only one salary, whether it is the husband or the wife that works outside the home.

Sometimes the problem you think you're going to have isn't the one that surfaces! Some couples have to overcome location problems when they find themselves in love while living and have careers in different states. Other couples need to live abroad because of their jobs or are assigned to a foreign country by the government for several years, which for obvious reasons puts a lot of strain on their marital commitment.

The career of one Irish-American required him to live on the west coast of Ireland for five years. He was very excited about the assignment, as were his three grammar school children. His wife, who didn't have a drop of Irish blood in her veins, wasn't so thrilled to be uprooted at 35 years of age and integrate into a foreign culture. She worried about how the children would be accepted and if they would fit in with children in a local country school in Ireland. Within one month all three children became integrated into the school. Several of the local children came over to meet the mom and to teach their new American friends from over the waters how to play Irish games like hurling and Irish football.

The husband also remained very excited about the whole experience. However, the wife, who brought expectations like taking clothes to the cleaners for one-hour service and having her nails manicured weekly, complained to her husband that she couldn't stand the poor service in the little nearby village. Unfortunately, her husband hadn't studied much about communication in marriage or taken any courses in psychology. Rather than actively listening and empathizing with her disappointment, he criticized her before the children and caused her to withdraw into deep depression for two months.

Whatever circumstances jeopardize the commitment of a couple or the maintenance of a good marriage, it behooves the couple to have extremely good communication skills and an ability to support each other in resolving the issues. In most circumstances it means putting the marriage before a person's career. This may be a very daunting task, particularly for ambitious executives or politicians. Some of us who live on the East Coast of the US are aware of at least one fine statesman who refused to run for president of the United States, even though his party wanted him to run, because his wife felt emotionally incapable of handling the pressure of being first lady in America. I have a lot more respect for that individual for putting his marriage ahead of a chance to run for the most prestigious job in the world.

A final question is "what steps do couples need to take at the beginning of a marriage to guarantee as far as possible the success of their marriages?" In my own situation I had to make a professional adjustment. When Laurie and I were discussing our goals and vision for a happy marriage, she asked me "Finbarr, how many nights do intend to see clients?"

Being a little anxious to be seen as a hardworking therapist and wanting to earn my share of income to pay rent and living expenses, I said "Laurie, you know that most of the clients I see are couples and many are not free to come during the working day. I would like to be able to see clients on every weekday evening."

It didn't take her long to reply with "Why should I marry if I am only going to see my husband on weekends?" Although I was a little taken back by her response, we did work out a good compromise. We agreed that I would limit my irregular hours to Monday and Tuesday evenings and Saturday mornings. It didn't seem to have a negative effect on my practice, and Laurie was quite happy with the income I took home each month.

This solution helped us quickly decide how to divide the responsibilities in our home. Related to cooking, for example, Laurie agreed to cook on weekends, while I would cook dinner on Wednesdays, Thursdays and Fridays. We even took turn cooking for guests, with Laurie cooking if the particular guests were primarily friends of mine and vice versa if the guests were Laurie's friends or family.

Some other issues that develop during the marriage will also test the commitment of at least one of the parties. Mindful of the vows that couples make on their wedding day, "for better or worse, for richer or poorer, until death do us part," nobody wishes for the worst to happen but, to quote Murphy's Law, "If anything can go wrong, it will." Negative issues do surface and can threaten the very foundation of the marriage.

I am reminded of one couple who had five beautiful children. The husband had several addictions that did not surface until several years into the marriage. It began to become evident when the husband started having job difficulties and started excusing himself to stay out at night, supposedly to meet clients. His wife naturally became suspicious and started checking his calendar in his briefcase and the items in his wallet. On one occasion she was shocked to see the picture of one of her former girlfriends in her husband's wallet. When she confronted him, he confessed that he had been having an affair for two years. In the counseling sessions that followed, he actually admitted that he felt relieved to be caught. What surfaced was a full-blown midlife crises aggravated by a double addiction to sex and alcohol. He was fortunate to have married a very secure woman who stood by her man and helped him monitor his addictions in a manner they could both live with.

Some observers may argue that marriage should not be the permanent commitment that society and major religions defined it to be at a time when people didn't live for more than forty or fifty years. With average life expectancy now approaching 80 in many Western societies, those people who have had a series of monogamous marital relationships over the years argue that, because so many people get divorced anyway, marriage to one person for a lifetime should not be assumed as the ideal.

In my opinion, such rationalization does not take into account the negative effects that divorce has on the children's emotional well being. It also ignores how individuals bond and grow precisely because they know that marriage is 'til death do us part. A final word from Leo Buscaglia: "Life is a trip; Life is the process; Life is getting there." Alternatively, as I've explained in other writings, "A wedding is a day; a marriage is a lifetime."

Chapter 7
A Pampered Child Makes a Pampered Spouse

A few years ago I was counseling another young couple, both of whom had been born in India. The parents of the prospective bride and groom had arranged the marriage. During the initial interview, the wife professed that their families were from the Brahmin caste and that in her judgment their families were compatible. Her husband, an engineer, disagreed adamantly, saying that she belonged to a lower caste and added, "It is clear to me that she is an example of "a pampered daughter makes a pampered wife." The "mistake" he saw his wife making was that she was not being the subjective, docile wife to him that his mother had been to his father. In fact, when his father died prematurely and he took over as head of his family, he dominated his own mother so badly that she warned her prospective daughter-in-law of the dangers involved in marrying her son.

After they had been married for about two years, they decided to immigrate to the US because there were many more job opportunities there for a man who had superior skills in computer technology. His bride waited on him hand and foot for the first few years after they came to America, and he was very happy. He was also very excited when she bore him a son and foolishly expected that she would quit working and be a stay-at-home mom. Focused only on his own career as a successful computer consultant, he hadn't noticed his wife's growth both professionally and socially. With a Master's degree in business, good people skills and part of a minority, she had climbed the corporate ladder very quickly during their years in the US. She took to the American way of life like fish to water and, through socialization at work, developed many of the habits of dress and personal appearance of the modern day American professional woman.

Her refusal to take time off from her career to take care of their son made him very angry and he also felt very threatened by her confronting him. He abruptly ended one of the interviews by angrily saying, "You see what I mean; she is now a pampered wife."

After that I changed from counseling them as a couple to suggesting individual counseling for him. I had to help him make the transition from traditional Indian husband to contemporary American husband who would learn to accept the woman his wife had become in the "new" world.

Experiences like that helped me prepare for my future marriage to Laurie. I had already realized that she would not be the submissive, passive wife who would leave all family and marital decisions to her husband. She was already a confident professional woman with a great work ethic. She was neither a spoiled daughter and from what I could observe would not enjoy being a totally spoiled wife. She had already come a long way since graduation from college in Kansas. We both laughed when she told me her first job at Southwestern Bell was supervising 20 workmen climbing telephone poles in Kansas. She was already a seasoned manager of one of AT&T's projects in New Jersey, while I was struggling to reshape myself as a lay minister to people to replace my fulfilling ministry in the priesthood.

While discerning my future together with Laurie, I had to look myself in the mirror and ask honestly whether, because I had been pampered so much in the priesthood, I would have unrealistic expectations of Laurie after our marriage. It is true that during my days as a priest I had been put on a pedestal, especially during the ten years I headed a diocesan agency, with 1,500 volunteers and a staff of eight people at my disposal.

Even though as pastor I had subsequently become more of a team player and was less on a pedestal, I still had housekeepers and secretaries to wait on me hand and foot. I knew that I would be shedding most of these luxuries when I married Laurie. To make certain that both of us had realistic expectations of each other and were not carrying any unnecessary negative baggage into the marriage, we decided to schedule some interview session with a Christian marriage counselor. We took some standard psychological tests to determine if there were any issues like unresolved anger or addictions that might negatively affect the marriage. (Fortunately, there were none.)

On our third visit, the therapist asked both of us, "Which of you is going to be head of the family?"

I think he expected Laurie to say, "Oh, Finbarr is going to be head, as he is the husband" but instead she answered, "Doctor, with all due respect, we will share the leadership."

He tried to explain the Scriptural reason for his question, but not only did he fail to convince Laurie but he also lost both of us as clients. When choosing him as a counselor, we hadn't stopped to consider that this fundamental difference in perspective would disrupt what otherwise might have been an even richer probing by us into our relationship.

Ideally, he would have been more sensitive and not have posed questions based on his ideology. We perhaps should have taken a bit more time to choose a counselor less grounded in a conservative Biblical approach different than ours. When there is a good fit between a couple and their counselor, deep and early discussion in a supportive environment about sensitive topics such as sexuality, family planning and other potential issues can be very helpful in avoiding serious conflict after the marriage is underway. The deeper understanding and appreciation that results can also reinforce the commitment to the partner as a unique individual.

Another issue that affects a person's ability to make and keep a commitment is how comfortable each of the parties feels "in their own skin." The author Leo Buscaglia, in describing a loving person, writes, "I believe that probably the most important thing is that this loving person is a person who loves himself."

Later he adds, "I am talking about a person who loves himself as being someone who realizes that you can only give away what have." He encourages his young college students to develop to their full potential in education, versatility and creativity; and then to give it all away, saying, "The only reason you have anything is to give it away."

In the seminary in Ireland, our spiritual director used to say to us, *"Nemo dat quod non habet,"* translated, as "You cannot give what you don't have." The same statement applies to marriage. You cannot make a commitment to love somebody in marriage unless you have a healthy love of self.

Part of my commitment in marriage involves learning new things from my spouse. As a priest and therapist over the years, I didn't spend much time learning how to appreciate art or go to museums. Laurie and I have visited art galleries and museums in Rome, Florence, Sicily and of course New York. I have also learned over the years that change and growth both add joy to living and fun to your marriage. Laurie and I have invested a lot of energy in new experiences like learning to kayak and participating in hobbies in which we can more time together as a couple. Prior to us being involved in doing recreational things together, I must admit I wasted many hours at the beginning of our marriage watching football games on weekends.

Early in our marriage, I discovered that Laurie had superior people skills and was a very successful at enabling younger employees that she supervised to grow in their careers. I encouraged her to continue her formal studies and get a Master's degree in Human Relations. Ten years later, she is highly respected as a consultant in leadership and organizational development.

Similarly, when I started writing as a hobby a few years ago, Laurie was very encouraging, saying encouragingly, "Finbarr, I know you have several books in you because of your many years as a marriage and family therapist. People will enjoy reading them just as they enjoyed reading your autobiography *A Kid from Legaginney.*"

Eighteen years into our marriage, Laurie and I enjoy pampering each other in many ways. We spend many hours recreating together. Laurie comes with me to visit my folks in Ireland and I go with her to visit her family in Kansas. Because Laurie is very close to her mom and is concerned about her living alone during the cold winters in Kansas, her mom joins us for the winter months in sunny Florida.

There is an old saying that "Flexible people never get bent out of shape." Over the years I have often had clients whose principal complaint was, "Dr. Corr, my wife wasn't like this when I married her. She has become too independent, and it is driving me crazy."

My first impulsive response, which I learned to repress, was "Alleluia, thank God she is different." Instead, I would be more sensitive and say, "John, you expected Mary to remain the same sweet little innocent young woman you married almost forty years ago. Now is your chance to embrace change and to celebrate the wonderful "new" individual waking up beside you each morning in bed and blooming right in front of your eyes."

Each partner, whether man or woman, is not only capable of change, but an investment in life is an investment in change. The couples who are more successful in marriage set up a culture between them that not only accepts change but also encourages it.

Chapter 8
Cherish Her and Feed Him

When I would ask my clients, who were wives or young brides to give me one word to describe how they wanted to be treated by their partner or husband, many women would say, "I want to feel cherished." This is not a word men would use. They might want to hear "I want you to feed me and make love to me."

While dating a woman, you don't really give up your independence. Getting married or moving into her apartment, sharing the one bathroom, the one bed and two closets would be a different kettle of fish altogether. When I saw Laurie making sacrifices from the very beginning of our marriage like giving up half her closet space for me, I began to experience what I had being preaching for years to engaged couples: marriage is about sacrificing some of your own needs to make life and loving easier for your spouse.

Laurie was smart enough to recognize that. While I was still struggling with my transition from single life to married life, she was very clear what her role was going to be in relationship to me. As I reported earlier, when Mike Gerson asked her, "Laurie what are you going to do on Sunday mornings when Finbarr will be missing all the affection and admiration of his parishioners?" she just smiled and said, "Nothing! He is welcome to keep all the friends he has and I will invite whatever priest friends he wishes for dinner."

Learning to be sensitive to the other's needs and schedule turned out to be an on-the-job learning experience for me. During the first couple of months into our marriage, two of my best lay friends invited Laurie and me over for dinner. The need for personal affirmation from these good friends took immediate precedence over everything else. Because I knew that Laurie had no specific plans for Friday evening, I spontaneously said,

"That would be great. What time would you like us to come over?"

When I announced to Laurie that we were going over to have dinner with these good friends on Friday evening, once again her reply shocked me. "Who said I said I was free Friday evening? You just cannot presume to make appointments for the two of us without asking me first if I would even like to have dinner with them!"

I admitted, "Honey, you are right. I have to remember that there are two of us and involved in these commitments." From then on, I learned to say in reply to similar invitations, "Yep, that would be great to have an evening with you, but I need to check with Laurie first and see if she had anything on her calendar."

Several years ago, I attended a workshop given by a Californian psychologist named Neil Jacobsen. Having done a lot of research on what makes a marriage a success, he had written several books and spent several years giving workshops on the topic. On this particular morning, he told a packed conference room that what makes a good marriage better was when a married couple, especially a young couple, moves from being two independent "married singles" living together to being interdependent persons whose love continues to grow richer and deeper over the years.

We were all a little surprised to hear him say, "I give my couples written homework asking them to each write a series of "I will" statements of things they plan to do to make life happier and more fulfilling for their spouse."

He then reversed the process for the second week and asked the couple to write another set of requests. This time the statement was "I would also like you my spouse to do 'x,'" which would include action items that he or she had not included in their "I will" statements.

When I used these exercises in my own counseling practice, I found the couples actually laughing more and complimenting each other. One of the wives actually said, "Dr. Corr, I cannot believe that you actually got my husband to agree to cook a dinner one night a week."

I replied, "Correction dear, I didn't get him to do anything. He volunteered to do that as he knew that it was something that would please you."

I always reminded the couples of two things: that they alone were responsible for seeing that they kept their commitments, and that it was not the duty of their spouses to remind them when they were failing. What surprised me at times was that several people in the group did not know their spouse's needs that well or sometimes exaggerated some of their needs.

One young woman wrote, "I will make fresh pizza for you every Friday night." Her husband replied immediately, "Honey, you know I love pizza, but once a month would be sufficient."

Another young couple had trouble with the husband's controlling Italian mother, who wanted to see her grandchildren more than once a month. The Irish daughter-in-law wrote, "I will take our two children to visit their grandmother in Morristown twice a month."

Her statement practically knocked her husband of the couch with surprise. "You will?" he asked. "Isn't that what you want?' she said with a little grin.

"Well . . . yes," he said with a smile from ear to ear.

I decided, without telling Laurie, to practice these exercises as a husband. I recognized early on that she is not the easiest person to buy gifts for. Even my humorous gift on our first Christmas together missed the mark.

I do know was that Laurie was, and remains, very devoted to her family. I knew that any love and affection I showed her family would be deeply appreciated. Laurie's family was not only nice to me and accepting of my joining the family, but they were also generous and charitable to indigent people and charitable causes. Thus, it was a very easy task for me to be kind to them.

On one occasion when Laurie's mom and sister Michelle were visiting, even though I had put in my day's work, I headed straight for the kitchen to cook a delicious lamb dinner that would be waiting as a surprise when they all returned from a long day at the New York City museums. As time passed, I made it a habit to call my father-in-law once a month to chat with him and tease him about the political state of the country. To get the fun going, I only needed to tell him that Hillary Clinton's poll numbers were up. I would sometimes call my mother-in-law but not as frequently, as it meant going through a relay operator to cope with her hearing impediment. Since my father-in-law's death in 2003, I have made it a routine to send weekly humorous e-mails to my mother-in-law.

Another way of letting your spouse know that you cherish her is to think of a one-time act that you can do that has the effect of saying to her "I love you" over and over again. After we bought our beautiful home in Morristown, although the previous owners had the front yard professionally landscaped, I decided that a nice surprise for Laurie would be for me to secretly plant 50 pink tulip bulbs in between the green hosta plants and flowering azaleas and wait for them to blossom the following April. You can imagine, I had a hard time keeping my secret from her and was very excited when fifty little green buds popped up through the dark clay.

Laurie, who notices everything, remarked, "Finbarr, come here I didn't know the previous owners had tulips." Wanting to appear very casual, I just observed back, "They do look like tulips."

A week later when those little buds opened and revealed beautiful pink petals, Laurie burst into the kitchen where I was reading the paper. "They are pink. You did that," she exclaimed.

I just gave her a very big warm hug and said, "Those damn Leprechauns, you never know what they are going to do while you are asleep."

As Neil Jacobsen reminded the therapists in New York, man's needs in marriage are more basic. He needs a partner who feeds him and nourishes his ego. While he is now more conscious of the division of labor in the home, frequently taking his turn fixing dinner and vacuuming the living room, he expects his wife, and the whole family for that matter, to show their appreciation.

He relishes his wife and children telling him how proud they are of his accomplishments in business and on the golf course as well. As I have told many bride clients, in a sort of humorous way, if you want to understand your husband's needs, start first by thinking of him as a little boy in an adult suit. Shower him daily with praise. Celebrate his successes with family dinners; allow him the time to withdraw into his cave to watch a baseball game or a golf championship.

As we will see in the next chapter, feeding him involves not just food but meeting his sexual needs as well. Sex therapists will tell you that a happy husband is the one who leaves a table filled with his favorite food and is loved in bed by his favorite woman.

Chapter 9
Knowing about Sex and Romance

While growing up in Legaginney nobody talked about sex. Until I was I was about ten years old, I believed that babies came in the leather bag that hung on the back of Miss Day's bicycle. Miss Day was the local nurse who delivered all the babies for the district of Ballinagh. However, if the little baby decided to arrive during the night when Miss Day was not available, my godfather's wife Mrs. Frank Corr provided the emergency service, although I do not remember ever seeing her ride a bicycle!

When I consider all the sexually stimulating commercials and programs of education in human sexuality programs that children experience today, I honestly admit that I was sexually illiterate for most of my childhood. When I was four years old, I became aware that the penis perhaps had some significance besides for urinating. Dr Arnold, our family doctor from Ballinagh, came out to the farm in Legaginney to check on Mom and the new baby that Miss Daly had delivered the day before. I remember being ushered out of the bedroom as the doctor conducted his dual examination. After about half an hour, while I was still hiding at the top of the stairs, the doctor came out looking for me and said "Finbarr I need to look at something." He went down on one knee and proceeded to take down my pants and look at my genitals.

All he said was "Hmm", and went back into the bedroom and closed the door behind him. Years later, I concluded that the doctor was comparing the baby's penis to mine to see if both had the same characteristics. The least I got from the encounter was that this little organ must be very important. I have no doubt that the early sex education of children in the home, followed by sensitive and accurate information on human reproduction in school, have laid the groundwork for a more meaningful sexual relationships in marriage.

I am sure that the negative experiences I had, as a young lad growing up was the motivation behind my spearheading Education in Human Sexuality programs in the Diocese of Paterson for ten years. In addition to working with couples who helped educate parents to be sex educators in the home, our Family Life staff provided training programs for both lay and nun teachers in the Catholic schools. Our goal was to facilitate these professionals to be comfortable with their own sexuality so that when they stood up in the classroom and described human reproduction and family planning to the children they wouldn't freeze but would freely use the proper medical terms without embarrassment.

At one point, we had a male gynecologist from Ireland who generously donated his time and talent in these teacher training and pre-marriage programs for the engaged. With typical Irish humor, he told a story of a couple who came to his office in Ireland, complaining that they could not get pregnant.

"When I discussed with them how they performed intercourse, I discovered they were trying to do it through the belly button and not through the vagina. He added, "Imagine the fun they had when I told them the proper way to do it."

While I suspect the story was just an Irish yarn with little truth, the doctor's humor served as a great instrument for relaxing his audience and ultimately taught them to be more comfortable with a subject that they were not accustomed to discussing with anybody.

Men and women approach sex differently. For men, the physical activity of becoming aroused, penetrating the vagina and reaching a climax was the ultimate pleasure. For women, making love is a much more emotional and mood-setting experience. A phone call from the husband in the office during the day can serve as a catalyst for the foreplay and lovemaking later that evening. I would frequently recommend to a young couple that they give each other full body massage to help them become more knowledgeable of their own body and their spouse's. In this way, they would discover and share with each other information about the parts of their bodies that were more erotic than others and areas that were very sensitive to touch.

In the same manner, in her book *Dr Ruth's Guide to Married Lovers* Dr. Ruth encourages couples to share their dreams and fantasies with each other as a way of communicating their needs to the other. She tells a beautiful, sensuous story of Barry one of her clients. "A number of Barry's fantasies or day dreams are about wanting to have a woman entirely, to envelop her.

In one of these fantasies his body changes form and becomes a big warm membrane, a blanket of human tissue that wraps her intimately and completely and moves upon her surfaces like a total massage until she murmurs with pleasure wanting him." Dr Ruth goes on to describe, in her inimitable manner, how in Barry's dream his wife responds with gusto to his all touching membrane as she cries out with joy and writhes, thrusts and struggles in their passionate embrace.

As a pastor, I had the job of sharing the most updated theology of marriage with engaged couples while the married couples on the Pre-Cana team discussed communication in marriage, finances, conflict resolution, child rearing and a host of other topics. I shared with the engaged couples that, in the words of Allen Petersen, "According to God's own wisdom and design, sexuality was ordained for the propagation of the human race, for pleasure and for the expression of that kind of love between husband and wife that nourishes true oneness."

Young couples were usually surprised when I told them that they themselves were the ministers of the sacrament of marriage and that my function on the altar was to be the official witness to their marriage on behalf of the church. When both partners in a couple were Catholic and wanted to follow church discipline to the letter, I helped them form a conscience on birth control that was in keeping with their own particular family situation while still holding respect for the objective norms of the Catholic Church.

On one occasion, Dr. Ruth gave the presentation on sexuality at the Pre-Cana in Madison. The engaged couples loved her literacy and openness. At the end of the evening, she admitted, "Finbarr, although I am not Catholic, I do admire the terrific job the Catholic Church does preparing their people for marriage."

Our Pre-Cana program at St. Vincent Martyr Parish in Madison was the best in New Jersey. What I liked about it overall was that by integrating the spiritual aspects of love-making with sound psychological and physical data, we got couples to look at their marriage as a totally integrated relationship, with God's grace available to help them through the rough spots.

One client, a relatively young man, complained that he was not satisfied with the frequency of his sexual relationships with his wife Margaret. He was clearly very angry and contemplating having an affair with his young secretary. I listened to his complaint for about twenty minutes and then patiently asked him what happens between him and Margaret after they have put the children to bed.

"Oh," he muttered, "she is a pain in the butt. When I am watching the Knicks basketball game she comes over to sit on the couch beside me and wants to make out and kiss and stuff"

I shot back, "What do you do?" "I push her away," he says, "that stuff is for bed not when I am watching the Knicks play basketball."

I promptly gave him a lecture on how Margaret was seeking some foreplay on the couch before they both went up to bed and completed the marital act. I emphasized the fact that since she was a woman she needed a lot more preparation time than he did before intercourse.

A month or so later he pulled me aside to ask, "Father Finbarr, how come you know so much about marriage and sex?" I just smiled and let him continue. "For the past month I have been inviting Margaret to come sit with me on the couch during the game. We cuddle together, I touch her breasts and tell her I love her and during the commercials I steal a kiss or two. As a matter of fact, a few nights ago the Knicks were way ahead, so I said to Margaret let's go up to bed, you have me too excited. I cannot wait until the game is over."

In her book *Sex for Dummies* Dr Ruth writes, "A very big mistake that many men make is to confuse romance with sex. Yes the two are linked but they don't have to be tied together like Siamese twins. You should act romantic even if you are not going to have sex with your partner." "Let me explain," she continues. "Stretching out the foreplay is certainly romantic. But if you only act romantic whenever you want sex, then these deeds lose their romance."

The key to a good sex life for all married couples is good communication about their sex life. Having counseled and educated thousands of couples over the past 40 years, I realize that is a very difficult task for most couples.

I have heard all the excuses like "We do not have time for that with four kids to chauffer around, or, "I have barely time to feed him much less talk to him about our sex life."

Giving women their due, times have changed for them in the past 20 years. Many women are confused with their triple role of wife, mother and employee. How often have I heard the question "Dr. Corr, who has time for romantic conversations?"

I usually answer honestly. "Before your marriage ends up on the rocks, I would suggest you and your husband get a baby sitter, take off for a night or a weekend to the woods and get some energy and enthusiasm back in your marriage."

Times away like that can not only be a time for renewed commitment and sharing of dreams, but it may also be the very tonic that is needed to let both feel they are the luckiest people alive to have such a wonderful partner for their lifelong journey.

My hope is that couples young and old will be encouraged to talk about their sexual encounters, share their dreams and fantasies, be free to give each other massages and experiment with different positions of lovemaking. As far as men are concerned they need to learn that cherishing their wives is the key to good sex, and that even the phone call during the workday can help maintain the romantic atmosphere at home.

Chapter 10
Using Conflict Creatively

I have no doubt but that my humorous and caring godmother Kitty had a big influence on my developing an interest in and respect for Bishop Sheen, a noted prelate in the 1950s who was the host of a very popular television program. I read several of his books that were available for us in the seminary library. One of his more insightful books, *Peace of Soul,* had a chapter entitled, "The Origin of Conflicts and Their Redemption."

Bishop Sheen attributed all conflicts to "our human nature," which I interpreted to mean that since we are all human we are going to have conflicts in our families and in our marriages. The big question always has been and still is, "How do we learn to resolve conflicts without impugning the character of a spouse?" The bottom line is that people get upset not so much because they did not get their way when the conflict was resolved but because in the resolution of the problem their feelings were not respected.

When teaching conflict resolution, I would use a simple example that most couples found humorous, if not ridiculous, but it seemed to get the message across. "Suppose your wife Mary approached you, John, before Christmas and said, "Honey, I wish you would buy me a green Mercedes like the one my girlfriend Susie received."

John, not being well off financially, would probably say to himself, "She must have rocks in her head." Not wanting to be abusive, he might say something to elicit her feelings behind the request, such as, "I too would like you to have what Susie has."

Observing Mary's body language, he discerned that he had actually mirrored back her real feeling to keep up with the Joneses. This first step by John is crucial to moving forward to a resolution. He has not rejected Mary by saying, "Lady, are you nuts . . . do you think you are married to a Rockefeller? Where do you think I could find $50,000?"

After a little pause he might add, "I have a bonus coming up in March. Maybe we could look around for a secondhand Mercedes, or, if you can wait until next September when I am turning in the company Mercedes, maybe we could buy it from the company. Unfortunately, it is not green. I hope you could live with it being beige."

You will notice in the story how both of them compromised and respected the feelings of the other. She did not hold out for a green Mercedes and compromised on the timing of the request. He made a big compromise, as he had not planned on such an expensive gift at the outset.

Sometimes I would tell the married couples to simply ignore the apparent conflict or use humor to deflect from a situation that could become nasty. I might say to a husband, "You know your wife doesn't get along with her mother; when she gets off the phone after fighting with her mom, she needs to fight with someone and you foolishly get sucked into an unnecessary and useless battle."

Why not say back to her, "Honey, I am sorry that she is so cruel to you after all you do for her." It may not be a home run, but it is better than getting into a fight when you have done absolutely nothing to cause the fight.

When Laurie worked with the marketing department of a big corporation, she had to interact with many chauvinistic bosses, which was very frustrating for her as she felt very strongly that the age of treating men as superior to women in the workplace should have already been history. After a couple of years of marriage, I got to know her moods very well. If she had a bad day she didn't just open the front door, she burst it open. On one of the Thursday fall evenings, my day off, I had a pretty good day on the golf course, was home cooking dinner, and waiting to welcome my honey home. She burst in the door with a light raincoat on and stomped into the kitchen.

I greeted her with the usual smooch on the lips. "How was your day, Honey?"

She gave me a curt, "Alright," which meant it was not all right at all. She stopped at the counter by the sink to read her mail. She looked at the sink and said, "There are tissues in the sink."

I kept quiet and said to myself, "That's number one."

A couple of minutes later, while still reading the mail, she looked at the floor and said, "This floor is wet."

Again, I remained silent and said to myself, "That's two." Finally she moved over towards the stove and said, "Why is it that when men cook they always spill stuff on the stove?

I said to myself, "That's three …don't get sucked into an argument." I walked over to her with a big smile and said, "Honey, will you go up stairs and change your clothes or do you want me to take them off right here?"

She gave me a look that meant, "You must be kidding" and went up the stairs.

I waited for a few minutes and looked at my fish starting to cook on the stove. Five minutes later, she called down to ask, "Do we have to eat right now; I would like to go for a walk first."

I answered, "That's okay. I can turn it off and finish cooking it later. Will you please bring down my sneakers?"

Then we started one of the half-hour walks that we usually took on such evenings. About half way around, practically speaking at the same bush on the way Laurie would start sharing her feelings. "I cannot take Jack Baker anymore; he is ignoring me and driving me crazy."

After a slight delay I would respond, "Laurie, I don't know how you put up with him. What did he do today?"

I did not know Jack Baker personally. All I knew about him was that he was frustrating my honey, who was a top class performer in her department and who deserved much more respect from him.

Once Laurie had unburdened her anger and frustration, we would arrive back at our home, she a new woman and I feeling good that I avoided an unnecessary fight. If I had taken her accusations of my being a sloppy chef seriously and shouted back, "Look here, lady, you should be glad to have a husband like me who cooks you a nice dinner three nights a week. Stop bitching about the sink, the floor and the stove."

We would have had a grand big fight. So now, instead of a minor battle, we would end up enjoying my tasty dinner of fish, have a few good laughs, and God only knows what we would end up doing before calling it a day.

One thing that I always suggested to engaged couples and newlyweds was to have a discussion about once every three or four months on how each felt the marriage was doing. Each couple would be instructed to be open and honest about whether they felt fulfilled or not in the marriage. Each party was asked to listen nondefensively as the other party shared their feelings. The purpose of this exercise was to prevent unnecessary conflicts.

Laurie and I first started this process was when we had been married about three months and were driving west for three hours west from Kansas City to her parents' home. After a couple of hours on the road and getting tired of the country western music on the radio, I said to Laurie in as charming a way as possible, "Honey, I would like to discuss our marriage if you don't mind. I want to make sure that I am being the best husband I can be. I don't know I am being that unless you tell me if I am meeting your needs."

After a few minutes of silence she began to list the things she liked about being married to Finbarr Corr - the humor, going to the movies together - and then she added in a gentle way, "I would appreciate it if you didn't expect me to be the extrovert that you are. You seem to get energized by crowds of people, whereas I need more down time and don't have the need like you to be with crowds of people."

I told her how happy I had been for the last three months and most of that was because I was married to the most beautiful woman in the world. I finished my part by apologizing for taking so long to make up my mind to get married.

Our first evaluation was awkward but now we do it routinely every six months, with a special session at the beginning of the year when we talk about mundane things like a family budget and any extraordinary expenses we foresee in the coming year.

On another occasion Laurie and I wanted to do something special for our tenth wedding anniversary in October '98. Laurie had agreed to make the reservations but seemed to be delaying.

When I finally pressed by saying, "Can I help? I know you have a busy schedule," she revealed the real reason for her reticence.

"I really cannot see me being away in October of this year, as I will be finishing my Master's in the fall and will probably have to do some kind of a dissertation at that time. Why don't you pick some other place we could go to celebrate and do it in July."

I answered joyfully, "Why not bring next year's vacation forward and go to Italy another year?"

Laurie looked at me in surprise and said, "Pray tell where were we supposed to go to in 1999?"

Without missing a beat, I said, "We had talked about going to Ireland and Scotland next year for a few weeks."

She responded immediately. "I am not in favor of going to two different countries on the same trip. Which country would you prefer to visit?"

"As a golfer, I have had this desire to visit Scotland and see the Royal and Ancient St Andrew's golf course for a long time. In any case I have been in Ireland since I was a kid".

She reminded me, "You know I cannot be away for several weeks."

We ultimately agreed to Scotland, staying at B&B's for ten days, not counting the days of travel.

When I use this example while counseling clients, I point out how we both respected each other's feelings. If I had talked her into staying more than the ten days, Laurie would have eventually been an unhappy camper. If she had forced me to come home after a week versus ten days, I would have given in but would have carried resentment for quite awhile.

On the following Christmas I might have been tempted to say to her, "Honey, I don't feel like going to Kansas this holiday. Why don't you just go alone to visit your family, I will stay here with the cat." This obviously would not have been a positive step to growth in the marriage.

Learning how to face an obvious marital conflict and negotiate a resolution that respects the feelings of both parties may take some time for the average couple. While we all feel uncomfortable confronting a spouse we love dearly, ignoring the conflict is not the answer. If we decide to push our feelings under the rug, not only is it dishonest but it will also come back to haunt us.

I have encouraged individual brides and grooms to learn to live with the uncomfortable feeling of confronting and initiate by saying something like "I love you dearly, but I am not comfortable with what you are asking me to do here." Sharing feelings usually will not get you in trouble, burying feelings will.

Chapter 11
An Affair is a Sign, but of What?

As a guest speaker at my weekly Rotary meeting, I discussed my book *A Kid from Legaginney* and referenced my friendship with Dr. Ruth Westheimer. The following week, at the same meeting, I over heard some older members talking about me at the next table, wondering out loud how I could be a good priest and be that close to the outlandish host of the show "Ask Dr Ruth."

I could not let that opportunity for a rebuttal pass. I grabbed the microphone and humorously confessed to eavesdropping on the conversation at the next table. "Bob and Harry are concerned that maybe I wasn't such a good priest, having had a close relationship with the outlandish host of "Ask Dr Ruth." I continued, "Since I am a new kid in the area I would like to defend my reputation." I paused to raise my right hand and proceeded to slowly say, "I didn't have sex with that woman Dr Ruth. I did have her on my knee four of five times but that wasn't sex". With all due respect to President Clinton and my friend Ruth, I brought down the house with laughter.

True, I did not have an affair with Dr Ruth, but I did learn a lot about the dynamics of marital affairs by listening to her insights and during my 31 years as a licensed marriage and family therapist. According to Dr James Spring, author of *After the Affair*, 37% of married men and 20% of married women have been unfaithful to their marital vows. Some of us marriage counselors would venture to say that the numbers are higher, knowing that a trespasser is as likely to lie to a researcher as they are to their spouse.

One of the most common forms of infidelity I came across many times in my counseling career was what I call the "Garden Variety." In simple language, the cheating spouse has an affair to get a message of disappointment across to their spouse. I know this sounds overly simplistic for a very complicated event.

The Garden Variety usually starts with some form of midlife crisis for men between the ages of 38 and 42. Later in my career I discovered men as young as 23 or 25 or rich young women living in the suburbs having a similar experience.

The 38-year-old husband is usually a career-driven, aggressive individual who is determined to reach the top of his corporation. He spends long hours commuting to an office, where a typical day is ten or eleven hours competing and working himself to the bone. Having reached the level of manager in the first 20 years, he fails to achieve the position of vice president that he had expected. Disappointed, maybe even heartbroken, he arrives home to share with his wife what he is feeling as a tragedy.

Not seeing the hurt of rejection in his face and thinking about their beautiful home and family, she fails to listen or empathize with his imagined hurt. "Honey," she says "you have done great. I am happy with the salary you make. We have a lovely home and three great children in good schools. What else do we need?"

This unempathetic response adds to his depression and he returns to his office feeling worse than when he spoke to her. As the weeks go on his female assistant, possibly a young divorcee, sees her beloved boss moping around the office and reaches out to him.

"You haven't been yourself recently is, there anything I can do to help?"

He hesitates for a minute and then bursts out with, "What do you have to do in this company to get ahead?"

His assistant is empathetic. "You are absolutely correct, sir; they should never have passed you by last month. You were much more deserving of the vice president job than the person who got it."

Mr. Reilly is hooked and feels understood, which didn't happen at home. The relationship with his attractive assistant grows from a desk side chat, to the cafeteria for lunch, to cocktails after work, to dinner and then to bed. Because of the empathic relationship at the office, he comes home his cheerful self, leading his wife to think that he is over the rejection at work, which is okay until she comes across a receipt in his wallet for $3,000.00 ring after the Christmas holiday. Since she didn't receive a ring, some other woman did, or so she assumes and goes berserk. Fortunately, going on the warpath for her meant calling a marriage counselor before a divorce lawyer.

When counseling such a couple, I usually saw the husband and wife separately in the beginning. I refused at all costs to meet the husband's lady friend, no matter how much he tried to persuade me of his deep love and satisfaction with the relationship. I would get the husband to talk about his life and career and about how he had failed to realize his dream.

Whenever I felt he was ready, I would approach the subject of asking how he felt about possibly reaching the pinnacle of his career at the age of 38. If he was able to resolve this fact and accept the idea that he was never going to become vice president of this organization, I would then proceed to reflect how his wife did not understand the depth of his pain and therefore failed to empathize with his tremendous loss and rejection by his superiors.

He would then understand that his attractive assistant came in to fill the vacuum left by his wife. If the husband happened to be a deeply spiritual man, I would interpret his midlife crisis differently, saying something like. "You have climbed the emotional career ladder with deep intensity for years, going as far as you can go in this company. It must be very difficult to accept that you are not going to make CEO or President. Having reached the pinnacle at this relatively young age, you begin your journey back down. You could interpret it as a spiritual journey and one filled with satisfaction as you journey back to the Father."

To move the husband to experience and empathize with the wife's anger took a lot of patience on the therapist's part. After several sessions, the wife would usually be prepared to acknowledge that her husband leaving the receipt in his wallet for her to find was a way of telling her, "I need you. I am hurting."

The wife has the choice of playing victim, staying angry or beginning the process of healing and forgiveness. Once they both reach the stage of recognizing that the affair was symptomatic of their inadequate relationship, the real marriage therapy of building an open and trusting relationship can begin.

The husband needs to commit himself to ending the affair even if that means he or his girlfriend changing jobs. For the wife to begin the healing process, she needs almost physical proof that the affair is finished. The reality is that the affair may have done both of them a favor, because their marriage up to that point was only a mere arrangement between two people living together, having children, but never developing a relationship where they resolved conflicts, expressed anger, identified patterns of conflict avoidance, or shared deep pain.

I was never that naïve as a therapist to say to both of them together, that the affair was a blessing for them. If I did, I am certain some of those wives would scream at me, "Has your wife ever been unfaithful to you, Dr. Corr?"

I was once asked by a client, "How would you feel, Dr. Corr, if Laurie had an affair?" Being honest, I replied, "I would be angry at first and then I would feel bad, as I know the guilt would be killing her."

Knowing that no one can ever say "never," I do believe that people with values and self confidence like Laurie are not likely to be seduced by the affection of needy men, who are either afraid of intimacy or afraid to be vulnerable with their own partner. I have had clients who were so afraid that they would choose instead to have a quickie sexual encounter with a third party. Such an individual can be helped in therapy, and the marriage can be saved if the person is prepared to face up to his or her fears and learn to trust their spouse, become vulnerable to each other and be nonpunitive.

Deciding whether to recommit or quit is an important second step once the affair has been acknowledged. In the latter instance, the affair was just an excuse to end the marriage. They knew from the beginning that once the affair became public their assertive, punitive wives would never forgive or get on with the relationship. I remember counseling such a couple where the timid husband had an affair 25 years previously. The spouse didn't let him forget for a minute. After listening to her tirade of chastisement for nearly an hour, I asked her what it would take for her to forgive her husband and get on with the marriage.

She looked at me as if I had two heads and said, "I thought that you a former priest would understand and punish him for his sins. I can see that you are just like the other three therapists we have seen. You don't get it."

She walked out and never came back and didn't pay my fee either. Her beaten-down husband just looked at me and apologized for wasting my time. He said, "She will never get over it. I already have decided that I need to move out and get on with my life." I call affairs like that "out the door" affairs.

Another category of marital infidel I met in the course of my years of counseling was the sexual addict. These clients, usually men, had a series of affairs and monogamous relationships. Being emotionally damaged as children, they were forever seeking the unfulfilled love from childhood. Their *modus operandi* for life was "I want what I want and I want it now."

They were frequently attracted, and then married, to women who mothered them and learned to live with the husband's flirtatious behavior. These wives would become enablers of the husband's inappropriate behavior and become so dependent on him that they lacked the courage to tell the cheater "Hit the road, Paddy." Colleagues of mine who counseled addicts say that the serial cheater needs to face up to his addictive personality, as their problems were not usually confined to sexual activity.

I have frequently been asked, "Do you the husband or wife always have to disclose the affair to your spouse?" The obvious ethical reply is "Yes," but I must admit that there were several times when I gave the opposite advice as a therapist.

One young attractive wife had a one-night fling with one of her husband's fellow students. Since it was a one-night affair performed under the influence of alcohol, there was no emotional exchange or commitment to continue. Both she and her husband were practicing Christians, and attended a conservative fundamentalist church. Bothered by her guilt, she sought counseling from their minister, who insisted that she confess to her husband. She followed his counsel unfortunately. Her husband was unforgiving, even after his wife agreed to a three-way conference with her one-incident lover. He divorced her, leaving her with two children and a chronic physical disability. I would have counseled her differently.

I once counseled a married gentleman who attended a very conservative Christian church with his spouse. His infidelity involved going frequently to a massage parlor and sometimes accepting services beyond the boundaries of propriety. He and his young wife were struggling to have a baby.

Like the wife in the previous story he was determined to confess and get it off his chest. I believed that the admission of infidelity would crush his wife's spirit irrevocably. I probed the motivation behind the desire to confess. "Are you going to do this because you have difficulty putting up with this awful guilty feeling you have daily, or is it because the elders in your church say it is the right thing to do?"

He was totally stunned with my question and couldn't answer directly. Then I said to him, "You need to discern what is the first and most loving decision you need to make right now. You should break the habit of going to the massage parlor altogether or seek out a parlor where nothing immoral is perpetrated on their clients." I knew that the desire to confess to his wife was just a short-term excuse to be rid of the pain of guilt and not motivated by a desire to be a morally good person.

Several therapists, who specialize in counseling couples where a spouse has been unfaithful, maintain that confessing the secret is a nonnegotiable step toward restoring trust in the relationship. Sometimes the unfaithful person does not have much of a choice but to confess for the health of their partner.

One prospective groom shared with me in a pre-marriage counseling session how he had sex with a prostitute two times after becoming engaged. I told him that because of the fear of transmitting a communicative disease to his fiancé he had to step up to the plate and confess. I offered to help him by having him tell her in the next conjoint counseling session. She was naturally very hurt but didn't cancel the wedding. They continued counseling for two more months, and got married with renewed trust and openness in the relationship.

To bring some closure to this discussion, I believe that no two situations are alike. What is good for one couple may be bad, even destructive for another couple. For some couples, the truth can have adverse, even deadly consequences. For others, it's essential for restoring a damaged relationship. When the unfaithful spouse decides to confess, I do warn them that it is important that he or she be clear about their motivation and knows that it will take months of good communication and openness to help their partner heal.

As a general rule, I propose a three-stage model for treating couples recovering from an extramarital affair: 1) Treat the impact the affair had on both parties. The innocent party needs post-traumatic counseling just as for any other tragedy. 2) Examine the reasons behind the affair. What is the context in which it happened? That will dictate the on going counseling and healing necessary. 3) The "moving-on" stage calls for forgiveness and the development of new relationship patterns of regular "one-on-one" sessions on how to build communication and prevent future infidelities.

Chapter 12
Respecting Each Other

While contemplating my final steps towards my own marriage, I began to look at the best and worse scenarios that might take place. I was very conscious of the positive gifts I was bringing, like a good sense of humor and the ability to discern others persons' needs besides my own. On the other hand, I was very conscious that my quick Irish temper could be an issue to be dealt with. What if Laurie and I fell into a negative pattern that developed into an abusive relationship?

In my childhood, Dad was moody and Mom could lay on the guilt, but neither of them was abusive to each other, to me or to my eight siblings. However, one of my mom's helpers endured spousal abuse of which we were aware. I was determined never to be in such a marriage.

In my counseling practice of over 30 years, I have met wives who were far from shrinking violet types when it came to how they treated their husbands. In one case, a young priest I was supervising held the first meeting with a couple pre-categorized by our secretary as being "the average type with communication problems."

To my young colleague's dismay, this wife berated and screamed at her husband for the complete therapeutic hour. At the end of the session the young priest came to me and said, "I do appreciate your helping train me in marriage counseling, but I just cannot continue to counsel the new couple I met tonight. The wife insisted on controlling the whole interview and neither I nor her husband could get a word in."

I answered as affirmatively as possible, "Father, sometimes clients come to our office not to get help, but to create a larger stage, so that they may crucify their husbands or scream at their wives in a more dramatic setting. Let me see, what I myself can do with them next week."

At the next meeting the wife simply started from where she had left off the previous week, calling her husband a good-for-nothing stooge who was no help in the home, a poor provider, and a lousy lover in bed. Recognizing her need to vent all the accumulated anger, I let her tirade continue for about 40 minutes.

When she stopped to take a breath at one stage, I interrupted here with "Excuse me, Ma'am, may I make a comment?' She acted very surprised and stared at me.

Looking at her firmly, I said, "I don't know your husband at all, as you have not given him an opportunity to speak. You yourself are coming across as an obnoxious, castrating wife who doesn't see any good at all in this poor man."

Not certain what to expect next, I paused for a moment. Then I said, "Would you like to continue counseling with me, or should we transfer you to somebody else."

Her immediate reply surprised me, "Of course I want to come back to you. You are the first man in my life who has stood up to me."

I saw them for the next 14 weeks and helped create more balance in their relationship. It took all of my counseling skills to get her to actively listen to her husband. Sometimes a strong aggressive woman will dominate and abuse a husband unnecessarily. He can unwittingly be an enabler of this phenomenon if at the beginning of the marriage he allows his wife to dominate him totally. On the other hand, the husband may be lazy, and his wife does not have the proper communication skills to confront him in a manner that will cause him to change his behavior. By modeling how to communicate with her husband, the counselor can teach the wife a new and more effective way to treat a lazy husband.

Another woman left a permanent mark of her aggressiveness not only on her husband but also on me, her "charming and caring counselor." She was a large muscular woman, while her husband was a diminutive, prissy little man who always came to the sessions dressed in a bright red jacket.

In the course of their counseling sessions he admitted a past affair with their church pastor's wife. He claimed to have found his soul mate in this wonderful woman. He was in no way contrite for his behavior, which caused his dominating wife to go ballistic in my office. She spewed obscenities at him to no avail.

To resolve the stalemate, in my naivety I suggested that we invite in their pastor and his wife to a five-way conference. To my surprise, they both agreed. The following week I seated the pastor and his wife on chairs a safe distance from my clients, who sat on my couch with a big space between them.

I asked my little client in the red jacket to state his case. Then I said, "How do you propose resolving this obvious stalemate?"

To everyone's surprise, he looked across the room at the reverend's much more attractive spouse and said, "Honey, I love you and want to spend the rest of my life with you".

His own incredulous wife was audibly grinding her teeth and glaring in anger at the two now-admitted adulterers. The minister's wife turned ever so slowly to her husband, looked adoringly into his eyes and said, "John, I am very grateful for you forgiving my indiscretion. I promise that this will never happen again."

The minister grabbed her hand and tearfully replied, "I do love you and want you as my wife. I too promise to be more attentive to you in the future and not spend all my time worrying about the church members and their problems."

Those statements left our little red-coated friend out in the cold. Being unable to plead forgiveness, without appearing like a total phony, he just stared at the floor, looking completely dejected. His wife, unable to control her anger and the rejection, jumped up and startled all of us by taking the heavy leather belt of her winter coat and start belting her diminutive husband on top of the head with the big brass buckle.

He slumped to the floor and tried to protect himself by putting his arms over his head. His enraged wife was out for blood and unfortunately it ended up being mine and not her husbands. I tried to intervene by grabbing the mad woman's arms to pull her off her pathetic husband. The reverend and his wife didn't move to help but just sat there dumfounded.

Instead of letting go when I grabbed her arm, the angry wife turned around her head and bit me. She drew blood, leaving me with a permanent scar on my left hand. To nobody's surprise, the couple divorced, while the reverend took his wife's indiscretion as a wake-up call and reevaluated his priorities.

Spousal abuse, whether physical or verbal, does not have to be violent to be harmful. There are many subtle ways that one spouse can do emotional damage to the other. I have witnessed couples at social events being very insensitive and cruel to each other. I once heard a wife say openly in conversation, "We couldn't afford that with the salary Mike brings home," oblivious to how hurtful that statement was to her husband, a blue-collar worker.

Sometimes husbands think it is very funny at parties to say openly, "You guys are very lucky to be going home tonight and having fun and not like me, who married mother superior . . . Nun tonight, nun last night."

I remember one female client telling me that her husband behaved like that regularly, especially if they were out for an evening with two other couples. After several years of the same treatment, she wearied of his shenanigans and planned a comeback attack. Sure enough, his bad behavior happened again as they and the four friends were traveling home in his big Cadillac after a night on the town.

When he had finished his usual sexual tirade, she said, "Jack, I really don't know what you are referring to, since most of the times when we are trying to make love you cannot achieve an erection."

The other four friends were ecstatic with laughter, especially since Jack had no comeback. It was a long time before Jack used their sex life as the butt of his jokes again.

Some couples use sex, or should I say withhold sexual activity, as a way of hurting their spouse. I counseled one couple where the husband was a very successful businessman but was also very chauvinistic. His wife told me of one incident where she just returned home from the hospital with their brand new baby girl. She didn't have any domestic help this particular evening. She struggled to feed her two young sons while the new baby was napping. Her husband came home from his office and instead of offering to help getting supper ready for both of them, he settled into his chair to read *The Wall Street Journal*.

Hurt and angry, the wife was unable to say, "Jim, for God's sake, get off your duff and help me a little tonight." She had developed the habit of repressing her anger towards him and was using passive-aggressive behavior, such as not responding to his ordinary requests in a timely manner, to get back at him.

When I asked her why she couldn't share her feelings of anger and hurt with him, she described her fear. The few times she had expressed anger at the beginning of the marriage, he had emotionally abused her and she was very afraid that he might abuse her physically. One of the passive-aggressive behaviors she practiced was that, when they would make love, she wouldn't actively participate. She would just go along, lying there and refusing to give him the pleasure of letting him bring her to orgasm.

When she first started counseling with me, she was even afraid to let him know she was coming for counseling. The surprise to her was that when I had persuaded her to tell him, he came with the following week. At first he resented her telling the details of their sex life to another man and, worse still, a priest.

After a few sessions, he told both of us that he didn't realize that his beautiful wife, the mother of his children, was so unhappy. He agreed that they needed to create honest and open communication in the home and that he needed to do more in the home to help. Their sex life improved dramatically, with both participating and each achieving orgasm.

At times, he would slip back to his old sarcasm. One night, after a good sexual experience where she participated fully, he asked, "Did Father Finbarr teach you that too?"

The most common causes of marital turmoil are sex, relationship with in-laws, and finances. I have noticed in my years as a counselor that the spouse who earns the most money usually controls most of the spending. Other therapists say that the spouse who makes the highest salary also controls their sex life. Either controlling the money or withholding sex from the spouse who earns a lower salary can be an occasion of emotional abuse. If an engaged person, or a married person for that matter, feels that they are being treated as second-class citizens in the relationship, they should share that feeling with their partner.

No matter what happens in the relationship, there is never an excuse for either physical or emotional abuse. Laurie told me during our pre-marriage counseling process that, if I ever raised my hand to her, it would immediately be the end of the marriage. We both recognize that any two strong independent people living together are obviously going to hurt each other unintentionally, which is why it is important for each partner to be sensitive to any pain they cause their spouse. In later chapters we will discuss in a positive way, how couples can meet each other's needs, create fun and have a marriage filled with laughing and loving.

Chapter 13
Balancing Marriage and a Career

For most couples, there is no conflict between their decision to marry and holding on to their career. Unfortunately, this was not the situation between Laurie and me. Because of the Catholic Church's rule of mandatory celibacy for its priests, except those priests who converted to Catholicism from the Lutheran and Episcopalian faiths, I had no choice but to resign the Catholic priesthood, a career I loved. I contemplated joining the priesthood of another faith, as an Episcopalian or a Lutheran, but I decided that such a move would be too much of an obstacle for my family to overcome.

On the positive side, I was fortunate to have another career I could turn to. I already had a second career for several years as a licensed marriage and family therapist in the state of New Jersey. Therefore, I opened my private practice in Morristown NJ, just one month after my resignation from the priesthood. Laurie supported my decision to start a private practice and, in turn, I was there for her as she continued her education and changed her career to do things in life that gave her more fulfillment.

Other individuals entering marriage must also go through similar career or job changes, either because they and their new spouse live in different cities or because their full-time career is incompatible with having a family and raising children. Many corporations are employee-friendly and make a sincere effort to accommodate employees who for marital reasons have to move to a different state. Clients of mine who worked with Home Depot or J.C. Penney not only retained their seniority and benefits but also frequently transferred to the very same job in their new city.

Some couples are not that lucky. I knew one couple who had been married and living in the Midwest of the US. The husband wanted to follow the money and take a job on Wall Street in

New York. The decision was very stressful for both the marriage and the family. The wife, a stay-at-home mom, and the children were happy with the school and community they lived in. She had no desire to uproot the family, leave their happy home, and move away from her support system. Reluctantly, they agreed that the husband would take the job, stay in a hotel in New York during the workweek, and fly home every weekend to visit the family.

When they asked for my input re their decision, I just replied, "God bless you, if you can make it work, but as your therapist I wouldn't recommend it."

For such a couple I recommend that not only should they place a lot of emphasis on their communication, but also that every month or so the wife should take a trip to New York just to spend quality time with her husband. It is unfortunate and I do believe that such individuals put their career before marriage and family commitments.

A more common marital problem that had career implications was one in which a very assertive, professionally competent woman married a laidback husband. His wife Mary was very talented in a particular field and was quite capable of making three times the salary of her husband, who worked as a night watchman. Mary was a sweet woman who loved her husband dearly and did not want to have him feel inferior to her. She repressed her feelings and stayed home in their tiny apartment for several years taking care of their one child and afraid of having a second, as their annual income of $20,000 would not cover the extra cost.

Even though their furniture was falling apart, she rejected offers from her parents to buy her a new couch. She said, "Mom I don't want to embarrass my husband by accepting charity from my family."

When Mary came to my office for help, I asked her why she did not bring her husband Charlie along. She answered apologetically, "I am sorry I didn't think it was necessary. Isn't this my problem? He is taking guitar lessons this morning."

Using some rational therapy, I pointed out to her that sharing her problem with me and not with Charlie was not going to resolve the issue. I kept the conversation positive, even affirming that Charlie was probably a very good husband and father, but that he needed to know his wife was unhappy with their financial situation. I persuaded her to bring him in for the third interview. He was surprised, to say the least, that his beautiful wife was unhappy. I pointed out to Charlie that we were not blaming him for the situation since his wife knew prior to their marriage what his employment and compensation were.

The end of the story was that Charlie volunteered to be the stay-at-home parent while Mary got a job making $56,000 annually. Not only did they buy new furniture, but they also saved money for a down payment on a little house, and five years later Mary had a second child.

I also witnessed another marriage where the wife carried the financial burden of supporting the family. After they had the two children they wanted, the husband lost one job after another. At first, the wife was very angry with him. He just kept saying, "Honey, what do you want of me? I am trying my best to get a job. It is not my fault that each company I join has to downsize within six months, and, since I am the new kid on the block, I am one of the first to be cut."

The couple were very religious and started praying about their situation, which helped allay the wife's anger and gave him an opportunity to discuss and resolve the problem rather than fighting about it. The decision they came to was that, until the particular industry he worked in improved, he would stay at home, take care of the two children, and have a nice dinner on the table when she came home from work. She was happy to go back to work and earn enough money to support the four of them.

The husband had a good sense of humor and kept instructing the children to tidy up their toys and have the kitchen clean when mom came home from work. He was insightful enough to know that the children would tell their mom about his behavior.

The oldest child enjoyed being a snitch and telling her mom a secret, saying, "Mom the house was a mess all day until a few minutes before you came home. I am not supposed to tell you."

After the children were put to bed, both parents would have a good laugh at the "secrets" being shared by the oldest child. Their evening would end with the wife asking, "Honey, what other little secrets do you have to share with me about today's activities?

In a later chapter, when I compare marriages in the Forties and Fifties to marriages today, it will be seen that the present system of the two partners working puts added stress not just on the marriage but on the children as well. In the old system, Dad was the breadwinner, while Mom was the heart of the home, doing most of the cooking, parenting and driving children to sports, the library and other commitments.

For today's family situation, I tell couples that the marital relationship should take a priority over childrearing and their jobs. This decision does not mean the couple spends most of their time relating to each other and making love, to the detriment of their responsibilities as parents and employees. What it calls for is creating the appropriate mindset at the beginning of their marriage in determining what is important in their lives.

As we have discussed earlier, the wife needs to feel cherished in the relationship to be a happy wife. One of the best steps to achieve this is to leave some time at the end of the day to allow the working wife to talk about her day. While it may all seem repetitive and inconsequential to a husband, it is a very important vehicle for working women to unwind before going to sleep. Some women may have difficulty getting started with the process of sharing feelings about their workday. They may be afraid that their practically minded husband will either laugh at them or judge them to be crazy, immature, or both.

The process of assisting your wife to unwind might begin with a statement as simple as, "Honey, how was your day?" Noisy people (like me) who talk a lot have to focus on active listening and not make the mistake of giving advice. The wife is not generally looking for advice even when she says she is. She just needs a caring, actively listening husband who is prepared to soak up all she is worried about and hear who did what to whom in the office that day.

Active listening means responding with your head, with your eyes and appropriate facial expressions. It means learning to reflect back what you think your wife is feeling as she tells her story. It may mean you saying something like, "Honey, you must have felt awful when he said that to you," or, "Honey, you must have felt very good to get such a positive review."

Don't ever interrupt her telling her story to compare her event with a similar event in your life. I know from experience, that this is one way of turning your wife off and blocking her from telling the whole story. Obviously this exercise cannot be fulfilled while watching television or putting the children to bed. I tell husbands that when the children are all tucked in bed and the dishes are put in the dishwasher, they should call their wife over to the couch, put an arm over her shoulder, and just let her unwind. Learning how to be an active listener and an empathetic husband make take several years to get it down perfectly even for experienced therapists like myself.

You may be surprised to learn that doing the reverse exercise with your husband is a more difficult exercise for you, his caring wife. Over the years I have learned that the average husband does not want to talk about work once he is home with the family. That does not mean that he shouldn't do so. It just seems to be part of a man's psyche to leave the job problems at the office. He is usually capable of turning it off by the time he has commuted home. With both parents working, he will usually have driving assignments to drop kids off for baseball practice or swimming lessons.

The wife may have to draw him out; especially if she notices that he is withdrawing from the family and spending a lot of time on the computer at home. The best way to draw a husband in to talk about himself is to start with a question about his favorite pastime or hobby. A wife might say, "You didn't tell me how you enjoyed your golf outing with Ed last week."

In spite of their protests to the contrary, men need to be affirmed in their careers. If they are not getting it from their boss in the office, they need to get it at home. Some of the weaker husbands may be tempted to seek affirmation from a female colleague at work. I had a wonderful professional man who worked with one of the major drug companies. He and his wife were very active Christians in their own church and attended services regularly with their five children. His career progressed very well for the first 20 years until he was passed over for the position of Managing Director. Being very disappointed, he came home depressed and after a few days told his wife, who failed to understand and empathize with his loss. He shared the story of his loss with a divorced lady at work who did empathize. An illicit relationship developed, and the affair almost ruined his marriage.

An easy rule of thumb for a caring wife to follow would be to pick an occasion, at least once a year, when she and the children honor Dad for something related to his career. It could be a small promotion at work or simply returning from a business trip or to celebrating a talk he gave at a workshop. He will of course protest and say, "Honey, thank you, but it wasn't necessary." Don't believe him. He needs to know that his hard work to support the family is appreciated.

The supposed war, initiated in the Fifties, between career mothers and stay-at-home moms is still going on with no particular winner in sight. Mothers with the financial freedom to choose whether to work full-time or stay with the children give very convincing views as to why they choose either way.

As reported in the *Palm Beach Post* in Florida, March 16th 2006, Mary Ellen Huff, a stay-at-home mom, says, "I believe that the breakdown of the traditional home in large part started when women started going to work and putting their children in day care and preschool."

She goes on to say, "While I honestly don't judge anyone who does choose to work outside the home, I have never understood why someone has children if they plan on having someone else raise them."

On the other side Meenu Sasser, 35-year-old attorney has no qualms about having a career says that she believes that you can be both a great mother and a great employee. She wants her daughter especially to have choices in life. "I want to her to know the value of hard work and the value of organization and not only doing a good job for her family, but for her career and for her community." She adds, "If I spend $100,000 on her education and she decides to be a stay at home mom, I will be supportive of that."

Researcher and mother Ellen Galinsky offers reassuring words for both camps in the Mommy Wars. She engaged the services of the Harris Interactive market research firm for a survey of 1,000 children about their parents' parenting skills. In her 1999 book *Ask the Children* she records the result of the research.

The children interviewed came from economically and racially diverse households. The children were asked questions like, "Are my parents raising me with good values? Are they making me feel important and loved? Do they really know what is going on in my life? Are they someone I can go to when I am upset?" Galinsky reported finding no statistical difference in the responses between children with stay at home mothers versus working mothers.

A very interesting result from a 1985 study by Galinsky reports that children answered a question of what would they change about their families. It wasn't that they would want more time with their parents, but the majority wished that their parents were less tired and stressed.

The challenge for married couples remains how to simultaneously balance being a good spouse, a good parent and a good employee. My vote as a marriage and family therapist is not to sacrifice growth in marriage at any cost. If the marriage is happy and fulfilling for both, the rest of your responsibilities will fall into place.

Chapter 14
Empowering Each Other

No matter how often couples heard about the importance of choosing the right marital partner and were instructed to analyze their courtship, years later they often come back saying, "But Dr Corr, I loved him and he promised to change."

The signs that your partner is or is not going to be dominating are usually there from the beginning. The dominating young man will try to control his girlfriend's free time or tell her he doesn't like her hanging out with her girlfriends.

One young man was so controlling and paranoid that he objected to his girlfriend, a nurse, wearing short dresses or short uniforms to work at the local hospital. Very angry with her outfit one evening as he picked her up from work, he yelled, "Diane, are you trying to entice the workmen here at the hospital to look up your dress?"

Fortunately, the young woman had the good sense to tell her mother about his anger and remarks, and together they put an end to the relationship. Away from his girlfriend, this young man was, to all appearances, a wonderful and normal young man. He possessed good people skills and was a leader among the teenagers in the parish. I suspect that he went for therapy following his rejection by Diane. Diane made the right decision, even if it was painful. Without intense therapy, her boyfriend had slim chance of becoming an egalitarian partner.

The tendency to dominate is most certainly not just a male characteristic. Young girls frequently learn to dominate by following in the footsteps of their mothers. This pattern of dominating females is understandable in cultures like the African-American, where for hundreds of years mothers had to be as strong as steel to hold one-parent families together. Fortunately, that system in the African-American family is changing gradually because of economic improvement, more education, and better role models like Martin Luther King Jr. and his wife Coretta. More African-American children now grow up in two-parent homes.

In other contexts when the tendency to dominate becomes prevalent without a justifiable reason, this should be cause for caution. The controlling female may signal her domination in very simple ways, such as being overly critical of her boyfriend's clothes or eating habits. If he doesn't keep her behavior in check, she will progress to criticize his family and his friends. She may even attempt to keep him away from his family and friends. In short, she is not accepting him as he is, but is trying to manipulate him into being what his friends would call "a total wus."

He may accept her domination for a while, because some young men are very malleable if they are participating in good sex and getting affirmation for their change of behavior. However, the caution to such young men is that the role of teaching table manners and choosing friends properly belongs to mothers, not to girlfriends. What guarantee do these young men have that this superior-inferior relationship is not going to continue throughout their married lives?

There are an equal number of dominating wives as their dominating husbands. When the female is the dominating partner, the abuse does not usually become public. The reason is obvious: an abused, psychologically castrated male is not going to complain to his colleagues at work or on the golf course and admit, "I cannot play cards with you tonight – or, I cannot play golf with you tomorrow - because my wife won't let me."

Unfortunately, the dominating wife does not stop with dominating her husband. She will frequently abuse her sons as well. Her husband has already made a decision that his wife's condition is either incurable or that he is a failure as a husband. He does not stand up to her and take his rightful role as co-parent of their children.

One abusive wife constantly complained to her girlfriends about, in her words, "the worthless, stupid man" she married. She would angrily claim that her husband Dave had no social skills, had no ambition at work, and lacked the ability to stand up to his parents or siblings. She complained about his poor salary, even though he had annual take home pay of $100,000. At social gatherings, her shy husband chose to be quiet and passive, while his wife dominated the conversation.

The reality was that, he was a wonderful parent who spent quality time instructing his son and daughter about life and encouraged them to be active in sports and cultural activities, which he didn't experience as a child. Once every six months or so, unable to accept her berating behavior any longer, he would confront her. Of course, she did not listen.

The children remembered their marital wars. Years later when their dad was being eulogized at his funeral after a premature death, their son said to me in tears, "Dr Corr, Mom always picked terrible fights with my dad, and now that he is dead, she is telling the world how much she misses him."

Her girlfriends attending the funeral heard the wonderful eulogies from Dave's professional colleagues and wondered if they were actually talking about the same guy in the coffin. They were totally unaware of his professional successes or the numerous awards he had received during his career. All they knew was that Dave was "stupid and didn't have any ambition to achieve the goals set by his wife."

Dave didn't marry the wrong woman in my judgment, but he should have stopped her in her tracks early in their courtship by saying something like, "Honey, this is who I am, I am not you and I would prefer that you would stop pointing out what you see as my failures because your criticism is very painful to me. If you don't like what you see, then we shouldn't marry." Unfortunately, Dave was too nice a person to say that.

On the male side, another husband was delusional and thought of himself as God's gift to the world. His colleagues thought of him as a strong leader because he was successful in business and a good enabler of employees. His office frequently had the highest sales per month for the whole company. He made frequent derogatory remarks at work about his wife's weight to his chauvinistic friends, who thought him very funny.

The truth was that Philip was a street angel and house devil. His lovely wife Josephine belonged to a church where the minister preached that women should be subject to their husbands. The result was that she never stood up to the weak insensitive individual who enjoyed dominating her.

When he came home each evening from work, there was hell to pay if the children's' bicycles or toys were in the driveway and if his dinner was not on the table. He would shout at the top of his voice from the driveway, "Josephine, what have you being doing all day? Couldn't you at least have the driveway clear when your hardworking husband comes home?"

Being both spiritually and emotionally handicapped, she was incapable of standing up to him. There was serious psychological damage done to their three children, with one of them developing a neurotic dependency on his father. The daughter foolishly believed that if she were nice to her dad he would not abuse their mom.

Philip's behavior did not improve. Emotionally immature, he saw himself as a cool guy and relished the title of being an ornery husband. One of his favorite things was to invite some of his buddies over on Sundays to watch a football game. He would sit in front of the large TV and, rather than getting up to get his own beer, he would holler to Josephine, who was busy getting the children their supper, "Honey, bring me a beer.

To no one's surprise except Philip's, Josephine divorced him as soon as the children reached high school. He remarried a few years later to a strong woman who told him in no uncertain terms, that she would not put up with his dominating behavior. That second marriage is an egalitarian relationship that has lasted 20 years. Meanwhile poor Josephine was so hurt and humiliated that she refused even to date, lest she meet up with another emotionally abusive man.

The goal of every young couple should be try to develop an egalitarian relationship from the very outset. As individuals, they do not have the same leadership skills; and each person in the relationship is attracted to the other because of some unconscious needs. If a relatively strong woman finds that her boyfriend is overly passive and too agreeable, this may not be a sign that they are very compatible. All it might mean is that he had a very strong, controlling mother and now is attracted to a woman who would control and tell him always what to do.

That is not a good foundation to start a marriage. If a woman discovers this characteristic in her potential spouse, she should force him to make to decisions about little things to see if he is willing to change. In today's world, with so many challenges, like holding down a career, raising a family, and keeping a home, a woman does not need another adult child who is unable to participate as an equal partner in it all.

Similarly, the overly dominant male needs to learn that not every woman he meets is going to be passive like his mother and allow men to dominate her as his father might have dominated his mother. If he finds himself in that position with the first few women he dates, he should see a competent therapist and learn to let go and become an equal partner. If he does not do so, he runs the risk of becoming a serial husband with lots of alimony to pay to several wives.

Achieving balance and equality in a relationship involves some work by both parties at the very beginning. Each party needs to verbalize their goals for their marriage and careers as a first step, and then the other party can ask, "How can I empower him or her to achieve those goals?"

Marriage is a team sport without winners and losers. Ideally, it is a win-win contract where both parties feel free to reach for the stars knowing that they have the full support of their beloved.

Chapter 15
Marriage: How It Was, Is and Keeps Changing

Recently I was chatting with a divorcee on Cape Cod, who owns a haberdashery shop. Mary and I were sharing how we both had multiple and quite different careers. She had been a corporate secretary before she decided to go into the retail business. All of a sudden, she blurted out, "I am tired of this business, I want out. I have a wonderful cat called Sam; if I could find a man like Sam, I would marry him."

For once, I was stuck for an answer and just said, "Tell me about Sam." As I left her little store with a promise to return one day to finish the conversation, I began to wonder what kind of a husband she was looking for, and what was wrong with the one she discarded. I will try to come up with the answer to those two questions in the next two chapters.

If my new friend Mary was looking to marry a pussycat of a man who would jump into her lap and purr while she stroked his belly, ears and long tail, I think she was born in the wrong century or she was going to have to wait a long time for her man. Conversely, if Mary had been born into the ancient matriarchate that flourished in Crete, Sparta and early Egypt, she would be as happy as a pig in mud on a hot day.

According to several sociologists, the women in these cultures possessed a lot of political power. The women determined the social position of the men they married and of their offspring. In those cultures, men married into the wife's clan and the children inherited their mother's name. The women represented the intelligent and competent part of the community. They held many of the socially valued positions. The men held subordinate positions as servants and assistants to feminine ingenuity. In the fantasy of my friend Mary, husbands were nice pussycats of men, only good enough to serve as hunters and soldiers but not competent enough to run a family.

Sir Henry Maine, writing in 1906, said that the establishment of private property was the downfall of women's dominance. With the birth of modern civilization, the dominance of men in society and marriage began or returned depending on how you interpret history. Women are once again breeders of offspring, cooks, and housekeepers and, in reality, subservient to the strong husbands, who protected their private property.

On the issue of sexual morality men were expected in the matriarchal society to be chaste, while women were given some latitude in intimacy with several men before they decided on the one they would marry. In or new "age of enlightenment" and contraceptives, the expectations are very different. Men, with traditional religious values, would like to think of their wives as being virgins until marriage. They will not however ask the question, as they realize how unfair their expectation is, if they are no longer virgins themselves.

This attitude of male dominance in marriage and in society was wholeheartedly accepted by the Catholic Church in the Forties and Fifties as a role assigned by God. Father George Kelly, writing *The Catholic Marriage Manual* in 1958, observed that "A woman wants to be dominated by her husband." He proceeds to blame the husband if the woman, his wife, does not develop the womanly characteristics, which he lists as "generally warm, tender, understanding and loving."

According to Father Kelly, "Only when a husband fails to recognize his responsibilities does the woman assume the dominant role." He condemns women who have become dominant and writes that "despite her innate wishes, Mother has become the boss in millions of homes. She often has the final say on the choice of car; she selects the furniture, and often the husband's clothes. She may select movies that she and her husband may see: she often disciplines the children, handles the bank account and pays all the bills."

The Catholic Church was not the only authority to endorse male dominance in marriage at that time. The following is actually part of a 1950s Home Economics textbook intended to teach high school girls how to prepare for married life:

"Have dinner ready. Plan ahead, even the night before, to have a delicious meal on time. This is a way of letting him know that you have been thinking about him, and are concerned about his needs. Most men are hungry when they come home, and the prospect of a good meal is part of the warm welcome needed.

Prepare yourself. Take 15 minutes to rest so you will be refreshed when he arrives. Touch up your makeup, put a ribbon in your hair and be fresh looking. He has just been with many work-weary people. Be a little gay and a little more interesting. His boring day may need a lift.

Clear away clutter. Make a last trip through the main part of the house just before your husband arrives; gather up schoolbooks, toys, paper etc. Then run a dust cloth over the tables. Your husband will feel he has reached a haven of rest and order, and it will give you a lift too.

Prepare the children. Take a few minutes to wash the children's hands and faces if they are small, comb their hair, and if necessary, change their clothes. They are little treasures and he would like to see them playing the part.

Minimize the noise. At the time of his arrival, eliminate all noise of the washer, dryer or vacuum. Try to encourage the children to be quiet. Greet him with a warm smile and be glad to see him.

Some Don'ts: Do not greet him with problems or complaints. Do not complain if he is late for dinner. Count this as minor, compared with what he might have gone through that day.

Make him comfortable. Have him lean back in a comfortable chair or suggest he lay down in the bedroom. Have a cool or warm drink ready for him. Arrange his pillow and offer to take of his shoes. Speak in a low soothing and pleasant voice. Allow him to relax and unwind.

Listen to him. You may have a dozen things to tell him, but the moment of his arrival in not the time. Let him talk first.

Make the evening his. Never complain if he does not take you out to dinner or to other places of entertainment, instead try to understand his world of strain and pressure and his need to be home and relax.

The overall goal is ... try to make home a place of peace and order where your husband can relax."

Okay, I know you are laughing your head off, but that is what was taught in our schools and churches in the Forties and early Fifties. Now here is the updated version for the woman of 2000 (with a little sarcasm included) . . .

Have dinner ready. Make reservations ahead of time. If your day becomes too hectic, just leave him a voice mail message, regarding what time and where you would like to dine. That lets him know that your day has been crappy and gives him an opportunity to change your mood.

Prepare yourself. A quick stop at the cosmetic counter on your way home will do wonders for your outlook and will keep you from becoming irritated every time he opens his mouth. (Use his credit card.)

Clear away clutter. Call the housekeeper and tell her that miscellaneous items left on the floor by the children belong in the Goodwill box in the garage.

Prepare the children. Send them to their rooms to watch TV or play Nintendo.

Minimize the noise. If you happen to be home when he arrives, be in the bathroom with the door closed.

Some Don'ts. Don't greet him with problems and complaints. Let him speak first, and then your complaints will get more attention and remain fresh in his mind throughout dinner. Do not complain if he is late for dinner, simply remind him that leftovers are in the fridge and you left the dishes for him to do.

Make him comfortable....Tell him when he can find the blanket if he is cold. This will really show you care.

Listen to him ....but don't ever let him get the last word

Make the evening his.......Never complain if he does not take you out to dinner or other places ...go with a friend or go shopping (using his credit card). Familiarize him with the phrase "Girls Night Out."

The goal ... Try to keep things amicable without reminding him that he only thinks the world revolves around him. Obviously, he is wrong, it revolves around you.

Now, let us get serious for a moment or two and allow me to answer the obvious question of how I would write the guidelines for the Home Economics class living in this millennium. For a start, I would do it very differently from the original writer in 1950. The class would have boys and girls together. I would have the girls do a personal inventory as to what they were bringing as individuals to the marital relationship. The boys do a similar inventory.

Instead of HAVE DINNER READY, I would have the first statement be ARE YOU READY? ... for a lifelong commitment to marriage; not marrying avoid an unhappy home situation, a previous long term dating relationship or because you are pregnant? Did your father dominate your mother and be so controlling over you and your siblings that he did not allow the family's participation in decisions that affected them? Are you emotionally ready to go from being an independent young woman to being an interdependent spouse? Will the decisions concerning finances, careers and raising children be decided mutually and equally with your husband? I would have the boys in the class ask themselves the same questions with special emphasis on whether they have a tendency to dominate girls they have dated in the past. While girls and women in the 1950s put up with it, the females of today do not buy into such treatment, nor should they.

PREPARE YOURSELF. Ask yourself during the dating and engagement process, can I be myself in my boyfriend's presence or am I always playing a role of being subservient and deferring to his needs while ignoring my own? Am I too passive emotionally to stand up and ask for my own needs? I would ask the boys the very same question, as boys who have had dominating mothers are frequently attracted to overly aggressive dominating woman.

CLEAR AWAY CLUTTER Here, I would ask the young girls to see through all the clutter of words and gifts from their suitor and ask the questions, "What is he bringing to the marriage? What is his family of origin like? How does he relate to his mother and sisters? Do you know how he treated girls he previously dated? Does he have a substance abuse problem?" This is probably one of the most difficult tasks for a young woman or man to accomplish. How many times as a marriage counselor have I asked an unhappy wife she married her husband in the first place? The usual answer I got was either "Dr. Corr, we were so much in love," or "Because so many people kept talking me out of the relationship, I was determined to prove them wrong . . . but they weren't."

PREPARE THE CHILDREN, Here I would have the bride ask her fiancé whether he wanted children and how many? Understanding his philosophy of child rearing would also be helpful. I have had too many couples come to me over the past 30 years saying, "We didn't discuss having children and now I am shocked to discover that my spouse doesn't want any."

MINIMIZE THE NOISE...I would ask the girls and boys to learn conflict resolution skills as part of their early preparation for marriage, so that when they marry they can avoid all the noise of screaming, name calling, etc. that are part of so many marriages today. For engaged couples, I recommend sitting down once a month and writing down three things they liked about the relationship for last month followed by three items they would like to see improved for next month.

When one or the other comes home from a tiring day in the office, this is not the time to have the one-on-one conference about their relationship. Each partner needs to discern the best way to debrief his or her partner's anxiety at the end of the work-weary day. For Laurie and me it usually involves postponing dinner, going for a walk, actively listening to Laurie, not giving advice on how a particular situation should have been handled. I have the angst, after listening to six or seven couples having a free for all fight in my office, all day while I am trying to help them straighten their relationship. Here the best way for Laurie to help me is to leave me alone and let me go to the yard and take out my anxiety on the plants and flowers for a couple of hours.

I know that that these examples do not necessarily apply to you the reader, who have two or three hungry children waiting for Mom or Dad to pick them up from the day care center. There is little time to debrief Mom or Dad. The focus necessarily for both parents has to be the children, serving them dinner, helping with homework, and getting them ready for bed. Even after all that, it is not too late to say, "Honey, how was your day anyway?" and then listen.

SOME DO'S AND DON'TS. Young men need to learn very early in their marriage about the do's ... i.e., to take home a little gift of her favorite flowers every week or two; send her an email to her office or leave a message on her voice mail saying "I love you." For the young bride . . . Learn how to inspire and encourage your husband in his career, making positive statements like Laurie makes to me "Finbarr, I really enjoyed the last chapter you wrote today. There was so much humor in it. Your readers will laugh a lot when they read it." A statement like that will mean a lot more than a positive book review.

One of the more memorable moments in my marriage was when we were married about a year and I had co-founded a company called Partners in Change Inc. Within a few months I got my first contract. I called Laurie at her office in New York and told her the good news. By 5 pm I when I drove home, I was shocked to see streamers on the door and Laurie's car in the driveway. She actually left her office in New York and came home to cook me my favorite dinner to celebrate my success.

Some Don'ts include…..Criticize the spouse's family even if your spouse has made negative statements. Don't discuss your wife's weight, her diet or the choice of dress she has chosen to wear to your office holiday party.

MAKE HIM COMFORTABLE … should read LEARN HOW TO MEET YOUR SPOUSE'S NEEDS. For a particular evening, it may mean the husband saying to his wife, "Honey, why don't you take the evening off and go shopping. I can put the children to bed." For either spouse it may mean surprising them by cooking a favorite dinner and celebrating the latest promotion at work.

LISTEN TO HIM … is okay, but should also include standing up to him or her when and if you feel disrespected or been taken for granted by saying, " I feel humiliated when you speak to me like that." If either spouse does not stand up and take ownership of these negative feelings, they will not retain the respect of their spouse and the marriage will not grow in a positive way.

MAKE THE EVENING HIS. I would prefer the statement to read MAKE THE EVENING A FAMILY AFFAIR where all hands get an opportunity to share the joys and challenges of the day. The youngest to the oldest tell their day's story. Mom and Dad can carefully listen and, with sensitivity, share family values. The evening might include the whole family going to cheer little Mike playing in little league or witnessing Michele make her debut at the school concert.

In fairness to the author who created the Home Economics course for the 1950 class, I do believe that couples do need time together without children, away from work, television and other distractions.

As a marriage counselor, I encouraged couples with small children to get a relative to take over the parenting responsibilities at their home for a weekend, at least twice a year. This leaves the couple free to go off to a quiet country inn to renew their commitment and love for each other. If the couple wants their marriage to endure and to grow, they must spend time nurturing it, or otherwise they run the risk of losing the most valuable thing they possess together, each other. Like the sign in my dentist's office, "If you ignore your teeth they will go away." Likewise your marriage.

THE Goal... The overall goal for married couples is to be conscious of their commitment to each other, and to be prepared to apologize and to forgive, because any two people living an intimate life in close proximity will unconsciously hurt each other's feelings or invade their space. The matriarchal dominance of ancient Sparta and Crete is gone forever, and similarly the age of male dominance in society and marriage should receive a decent burial.

Chapter 16
Have a Good Time!

From the beginning of our relationship, Laurie and I had a lot of fun. I know for certain, from my many years as a marriage and family therapist, that couples who play together do have an easier time resolving conflicts and never seem to get bored just hanging out with each other.

Sometimes it begins with the husband deciding to do a hula dance for his honey in the bedroom. On the other hand, he may come home from a late night at the office, having counseled several married couples and jump fully clothed into the bed on top of his wife and whisper in her ear, "Honey, you make it all worthwhile.

I believe that fun in marriage begins with an attitude. You can look at life as if it is a half glass of water and say positively, "it is half full" or be a whiner who sees it as "half empty."

Whenever I encouraged having fun, I frequently heard, "It is easy for you, you are Irish and naturally funny." My reply always was, "Yes, it makes it easier for some who have natural Irish wit, but that still doesn't ensure a home run every time."

The first Christmas I was dating Laurie I bought six pairs of panties and put them in six Waterford crystal glasses as a Christmas gift. She was very gracious in accepting the gift, but I discovered later that she was not crazy about Waterford Crystal period and also did not like anybody buying her clothes.

I don't always tell the about the greatest joke that Laurie played on me just a couple of years into our marriage. One morning, rushing off 17 miles to the office in early December, I forgot my upper dental plate from the water glass in the bathroom. Fortunately, Laurie was home that day from the office and came to the rescue. Doing her best not to embarrass me before my very serious secretary and remembering how I enjoy a joke, she wrapped up the false teeth in Christmas wrapping paper and dropped them off at the office with a statement to the secretary, "Wish Dr. Corr a Merry Christmas from me."

One colleague of mine made a book of coupons as a birthday gift for his wife. Each of the coupons was a certificate that she could "cash" at any time. One coupon was for dinner for two at her favorite restaurant. Another was a night at the movies to see a movie of her choice. His wife really enjoyed the ingenuity of the gift more than the actual value of each item listed on the coupons.

To interest young couples in the goal of putting more fun in their relationship, I would ask each spouse to discover their partner's favorite hobby or entertainment. It might be something as simple as the wife's enjoyment of shopping or visiting museums. The husband's recreation may include golfing, hunting or fishing. Even though I knew that men generally dislike shopping unless it is for something they specifically need, I would still advise the husband to offer to take his wife shopping every month. If a husband resisted the suggestion, I would ask him how much energy it took to go shopping on a Sunday afternoon when there is no sporting event on TV on that particular day.

I would press a little further, "Wouldn't you want to bring some fun into your wife's life by suggesting at least four times a year that you go together to the museum with her? You might even get to enjoy them yourself." This is only one of several ways to enrich the marital relationship.

In the case of the wives, I am not asking that they don hunting fatigues, grab a gun and go out in the woods to shoot deer, pheasants and quail with their partner. I do know of several wives who, although they were not naturally athletic, took golf lessons so that they could spend some Sunday afternoons playing golf with their husbands. For one golfing wife, the highlight of her month is when she and her husband participate in a nine-hole twilight golf tournament, ending with cocktails and dinner in the club restaurant. From a competitive point of view, while many men might prefer to play with men, most husbands will respect their wives' effort to learn the game so that the couple can spend more quality time together as they grow older. Based on the recreational opportunities available, the couple with a little effort can find a shared sport to bring more fun into their relationship.

One of my colleagues in New Jersey had a wonderful medical practice and was very popular with all of his patients. He was not very happy, however. He loved to travel but his wife would not go any place except to what he called "boring Florida" and, even there, just once a year. Whenever I would visit him, he always asked me, "Where is our "Sport" traveling to this summer?"

When my answer was Italy, Hawaii, or Ireland, he would just give a big sigh of envy. I have noticed over the years that couples who travel together, whether in the US or abroad, discover new depths of intimacy and communication that they never thought were possible.

As we discussed in Chapter 5, you just don't marry a person; you actually marry a family. Visiting one's in-laws is not always pleasant, especially if the in-laws are not nice people. Sometimes the hard choice has to be made to avoid an unhealthy negative situation and be free to do some fun things with your spouse and children.

I had one very warm, affectionate client who enjoyed having fun in her marriage and with her children. She had fun with her own parents and wanted to replicate this fun relationship with her in-laws. However, both of her in-laws were active alcoholics who, while they professed great love for their grandchildren, were always critical of their daughter-in-law. They blamed her for their son's not calling them or inviting them to their home. After years of trying and encouragement from me as their therapist, both she and her husband came to the decision to visit his parents just once a year. The rest of the year they were free to have fun with her family or just spending time with each other at home.

Some other spouses might be lucky enough to be blessed with in-laws with whom they felt a lot of compatibility. I had several male clients who complained that their wives kept running back home to their parents.

I usually asked, "Is she putting her parent's needs before yours? The answer was usually, "No" or "I don't think so."

I would then respond, "My recommendation is that you love your in-laws, if not for their own sake, then because your wife loves them and enjoys spending time with them."

This is just one example of developing a positive attitude toward supporting your spouse in something they enjoy even if you don't. You really can learn to love someone that you don't like if it's that important to your marriage!

I have met thousands of couples who enjoyed each other's company at the social events sponsored by their church. One of my earliest recollections of celebrating St Patrick's Day in Paterson, New Jersey, is of a woman named Margaret, born in Scotland but of Irish heritage. Margaret got up on the stage and opening the Irish party with singing "If you are Irish come into the parlor" while her husband Charlie played the same tune on the bagpipes.

I believe that their joy-filled marriage helped them to live into their nineties. They just enjoyed having fun together and sharing it with family and friends. Other couples developed a custom of inviting couples and having dinner parties in their home. They would split the cooking chores between them. She would prepare the appetizers, salad, and dessert while he cooked the meat or fish on the grill.

Having visited my in-laws in the Midwest a lot over the past several years, I have witnessed hundreds of couples having fun at square dances, rodeos and playing cards in Legion Halls and in each other's homes. They seemed to enjoy not just the dancing and the games but also getting away from the heavy work of farming to spend quality time as a couple or family with other families.

Near the ocean, depending on their age, couples can swim, surfboard or sail together, or just hold hands and walk the beach at low tide. Our neighbors in Florida have nicknamed a senior citizen couple living there as the "love birds." They go for walks and swim together, and are forever laughing at each other's silly antics. They come from different religious and cultural backgrounds. This has not prevented them from developing an attitude that marital life can and should be fun. They have achieved that by creating a relationship filled with laughter and love.

Chapter 17
Letting the Rose Bloom

Over the years I have witnessed all kinds of celebrations of marriage. One of the most memorable involved celebrating the marriage of two Chinese people. The bride and groom were fluent speakers in English, but the rest of their family didn't understand or speak a word of it. The challenge for me, the celebrant of the liturgy, was to give a homily that would be somewhat meaningful to the hundred or so Chinese guests attending the ceremony.

I obviously don't speak Chinese and, even if I did, I doubt that they would have understood Chinese spoken with an Irish brogue. I had to revert to using signs and symbols. I wanted the message to be about how love in a marriage will grow and blossom if the couple nurtures the relationship.

I took a real rose into the pulpit. After I read the Gospel, I hid the whole rose in the heart of my left hand. As I began to address the couple about how the grace of the sacrament would work, I slowly pushed the rose forward with my right hand and quietly allowed the big red blooms convey the message. I said nothing, I just paused and looked at the congregation for a moment and saw big broad smiles on a hundred faces.

Everyone got the message. Two years later a regular American couple came and asked me to witness their marriage. When I got to the part of discussing the wedding ceremony itself, the bride asked me if I would use my "Chinese version." I had already forgotten about it, but obviously, this young lady hadn't.

I don't know of any commitment we make that makes such a difference in our daily life than saying to someone publicly in church or synagogue before family and friends, "I take you for better or worse, for richer or poorer, in sickness and in health, until death do us part."

True, it is ritual, but more than that, it is a lifelong commitment that needs to be celebrated in a memorable way. In my first book *From the Wedding to the Marriage,* the emphasis, as in most of this book, was on preparing the couple emotionally for a lifelong commitment.

My goal in helping couples plan a marriage ceremony was to see it as a microcosm of their relationship and of their future life together. If, for example, both parties were particularly close to their mothers, it would be very fitting to have both mothers together light the wedding candle on the altar during the exchange of vows. Little nephews or nieces could be part of the procession to the altar, carrying the wedding rings or small baskets of flowers. A relative or friend who introduced them to each other or was supportive during the courtship could be invited to do a reading in the liturgy.

In American culture, the parents of the couple, usually the bride's parents are responsible for underwriting the cost of the wedding reception. I have told the bride and groom not to become overly involved or anxious about the reception party. Allow the parents to do their thing and invite their friends along with your closest friends to the reception.

The wedding ceremony and choice of the priest or minister who witnesses the exchange of vows is the responsibility of the bride and groom. As older people, like myself will tell you, not many couples will remember what happened at the reception unless someone relative made a fool of themselves by either drinking too much or saying something naughty during the toast. The bride and groom, however, will remember every detail of the wedding ceremony for many years to come. . That is why it is important to choose readings carefully – whether from Scripture or from secular books like Kahlil Gibran's writings on marriage - that reflects who the couple is both as individuals and as new partners in life.

Taking time off from work to celebrate a honeymoon is another milestone that you will remember for years. Where you spend the honeymoon and how much money you spend is secondary to the value of just relaxing and using the time to enjoy each other's company in lovemaking and deep communication. Planning a wedding can be very stressful, especially for the bride. She needs time to unwind after it all and just rest before she resumes everyday life. It gives the husband an opportunity to do endearing things like taking coffee to her in the bedroom as a small expression of how he will cherish her the rest of his life.

There are many stories told about honeymoons and honeymooners, some apocryphal and some actually true that are passed down from family to family. When I was a very young priest, one woman parishioner who was marrying for a second time explained, "Well Father, with my first husband, the honeymoon didn't go as he planned. He chose to insult me at our wedding by dancing cheek to cheek with his old girlfriend. Therefore, I refused to sleep in the bed with him in the hotel and slept on the couch instead. The next morning I came home and refused to continue the honeymoon. My doctor can testify that I was still a virgin, as I went to him for a physical the following week."

As she requested, her first marriage was declared null and void. At a private ceremony in church, I witnessed the revalidation of her second marriage. She didn't risk having another wedding reception since the first one had left a very bad taste in her mouth.

Years later I counseled a couple who married late in life and told me that they had had one hell of a fight on their honeymoon and had never made up. When I asked them to tell me about the honeymoon, the husbands story startled me when he said, "Father Finbarr, I thought we were going to have a good time on the honeymoon as we brought our pastor along with us for the holiday."

I suggested that a honeymoon is a very private affair, and that it was inappropriate to take anybody along, as that would change the whole atmosphere of what is supposed to be a romantic experience. I was able to patch up their relationship and they lived happily for next 35 years.

When I was growing up in Ireland, there was a beautiful custom of inviting all guests at the wedding back to a party on the night the couple came home from the honeymoon. It was called the "Bride's Drink." Looking back now, I thought it was a very fitting ritual that affirmed the young couple as they officially started their married life in their new home together.

I am sure that I am not the only married man to admit that the first year of marriage is probably the most difficult. Both parties are searching for space, both physical and emotional. Sometimes it seems as if the wife is trying to protect her space as the husband takes over one or two or her closets, not only with suits he uses for the office but with lots of sporting clothes, sports memorabilia and sporting equipment that she would rather see left in the trunk of his car.

He often would like to take a night off with the boys, but he is afraid to raise the question lest she misinterpret it and think he is not happy in the relationship. If she is insightful, she will recognize his tension and simply say, "Honey, it is okay if you want to go out for a night out with the boys."

At other times the husband, if he is an extrovert like me, will want to have loads of people over for cocktails and dinner, only to discover that his wife's tolerance for company is not the same as his. The most common complaint I heard from married women in their thirties was that they felt that their husbands didn't feel obligated to change their pattern of behavior with their friends while they the young wife was expected to stay home except for weekly trips to the mall shopping.

Most couples are able to achieve balance in the relationship between her needs and his needs in the first year. During this first year, they should agree on a budget and set a goal for when they will purchase their first home together. I tell couples not to wait until their first anniversary to re-celebrate the event of their marriage. Before they have their first child and even after he or she arrives, I recommend highly to all couples of whatever age that they go out to dinner at least once every two weeks. They need to get away from phone calls and television and have warm affirming conversations that are enriching to both parties.

In addition to celebrating birthdays and anniversaries, a thoughtful husband will celebrate their love by taking home a bunch of her favorite flowers every week or so. It adds charm to the relationship if either one remembers the anniversary of their first date and celebrates it in a simple way. Getting into these thoughtful things by establishing a pattern of romance and caring early in the marriage sets the stage for successfully meeting each other's needs and creating fun in the marriage.

Many congregations have celebrations of marriage in which they honor couples who have been married 25, 40, 50, or 60 years. A very effective way of celebrating the gift of your own marriage is to volunteer to participate in a pre-marriage program for engaged couples. As you are talking with other couples about communication in marriage you can be reminded of how lucky you are to have a partner that you can communicate with so openly. Your partner will feel very good when she shares with the group how cherished she feels being married to you.

The Catholic Church, along with many Christian churches and synagogues, encourages its members to participate in Marriage Encounter programs. Founded in Spain, this weekend program has helped thousands of couples throughout the world not only to deepen their communication through daily dialogue but also to celebrate their gift of marriage with thousands of others who appreciate the gift of love in marriage. It can help you remember that getting married takes just one day, but you should celebrate it for a lifetime.

If an engaged couple has a positive educational and emotional experience when they receive their pre-marriage instructions, this can be instrumental in their forming a relationship that continues to bloom for the rest of their married life.

Chapter 18
Growing Old Together: the Best is Yet to Come

Joe Carroll is 92 years young and an avid golfer. Even though I am 21 years his junior, I have difficulty beating him on the golf course. He and his wife Adele, aged 95, have been married 67 years and are as much in love today as they were 69 years ago when Joe stole her from her date in an ice cream parlor in Morristown, New Jersey. Joe visits Adele daily in the nursing home, feeds her lunch, and holds her hand. Frequently they reminisce about their life long marriage.

While Joe's mind is as sharp as a tack, Adele is bothered at times with dementia and will ask Joe, "Should we get married?"

Joe, going along with her question, asks, "What do you feel?"

She answers, "I don't want to be bossed around by any man, but I do love you and think we should get married and have several little ones. Do you think you are up to it?

At other times she will ask Joe, "How old are you"?

When he answers "Almost 92 ," she will say, "That is only eight years from being 100 and what then?"

Pointing up to heaven with both thumbs he continues, "I will go up there and wait for you." She responds immediately, "No you won't, I will go with you."

As Joe reflects back on his long marriage, he admits they had their difficult times but never threatened to divorce one another. From the very beginning they enjoyed each other's company. Going over to Sammy's restaurant in Mendham with five dollars in Joe's pocket, they would in his words "dance to their hearts' content." From the beginning of their marriage they discussed issues and made decisions together.

Money was tight in the early years, so Joe couldn't afford to play golf regularly. Providing food for the table and later a good education for their son Robert took precedence over golf and expensive vacations. Even in Adele's present state of mind, it is important for her to feel "we always got along real good."

Sometimes Joe will tease her a little by saying, "We did, because you were always the boss." Adele will give it back to him with, "Get out of here and go see your girlfriends."

His reply is always the same. "No Adele, I have only one girl and that's you." She answers, "It had better be that way."

It is no secret why Joe and Adele had a happy marriage for all those years. It all boils down to how they decided to live their lives. Making a lot of money could have been a choice for a young couple who had little income early in their marriage. Many young couples today make that their goal because they see wealth as the only means to having choices for alternatives in life. Yet sociologists tell us that most suicides are committed by the wealthy.

Joe and Adele didn't make the accumulation of money a goal in life. They instead chose happiness as a couple as their primary objective, and then to share the joy of their marriage with their child Robert. Putting an emphasis on joy in their family life became a stimulus to sharing that joy with other individuals and families.

One of the hurdles they had to cross was the Depression that hit the United States very soon after they married. While some financial investors were leaping out the windows on Wall Street as they lost their life investments, Joe and Adele continued to feel upbeat and resisted the temptation to become depressed and angry at the government. Joe chose instead to take Adele for short rides in his 1929 Studebaker Commander.

When I asked Joe to tell me about their wedding in 1938, he smiled from ear to ear. "I drove Adele to Atlantic City, New Jersey for our honeymoon with $50 in my pocket, $30 of which we received as wedding gifts." He added, "We didn't have a worry in the world The room in the hotel cost us only $16.50 for the week, our dinners were a dollar each and gas was sixteen cents a gallon. We had a wonderful honeymoon and danced to the wee hours of the morning."

The next challenge to face Joe and Adele was the start of World War II. Joe was lucky enough to get a deferment because he was working in a factory that made engines for the airplanes used by the US Air Force. As the war was drawing to a close, Joe was terminated at the factory and he went daily to play golf while waiting for a new job opportunity. His tough Polish mother-in-law was not impressed and challenged him one day as he returned home from a golf game. Adele and he had been living with her until they had saved enough money to get their own home.

The mother-in-law demanded, "How can you have the nerve to go golfing when your wife is working every day?" Joe replied that he didn't know and gave her the golf clubs as he added with a laugh, "I didn't ask for them back for 18 years even though I got a job in two months."

According to Joe, they continued to choose joy in their relationship over being angry and resentful towards each other. They resolved to solve problems, and shared both negative and positive feelings towards each other. Joe says that approach was key to preventing their conflicts from escalating to the level of a third World War. They both possessed a strong religious faith which they nourished by regular weekly attendance at Sunday masses and holidays of obligation.

Joe was a firm believer in keeping physically fit and, in addition to his regular game of golf, he attended the YMCA gym three times a week for more than 40 years. Since he learned to drive as a teenager, Joe had loved having nice cars. He would use these cars to taxi neighbors and friends to Newark International airport for a nominal fee.

When I asked him why he worked these extra hours, he would smile. "My regular paycheck is to support the family, the money I make on my side jobs pays for my golf." For his 90th birthday, Joe bought himself a brand new Toyota Camry, which he now uses daily to go visit Adele in the nursing home.

Unfortunately, I didn't meet too many couples like Joe and Adele in my Marriage and Family practice. People married 50 years or more looked at their commitment to marriage as an irrevocable decision. They took there vows for better or worse, for richer or poorer, until death do us part, to mean just that, until one or the other died.

When I asked super seniors like Joe their opinion of why so many people get divorced today, the answer often is that younger couples don't seem to understand that every marriage requires work and a lot of patience to be successful. Happy marriages don't just happen.

An older woman responded to the same question with, "Young couples don't make the commitment that we made. It runs right back to religion. For us there was no choice, you just stuck it out."

Another very important observation was made by a third senior who observed how the support system they had as young couples is missing today, saying, "Today we live in a fragmented society. We don't have close knit neighborhoods of aunts, uncles and cousins living within a few blocks. Today's families sometimes live thousands of miles apart, leaving young couples to cope with life's challenges and family conflicts with just their own resources." She added, "Young folks cannot handle it."

While I cannot argue with any of the statements made by my interviewees, I believe I encountered some additional attitudes among the younger couples I tried to help. In many cases the expectations of newlyweds today are very immature and short-sighted. Some might call it a spirit of entitlement, an attitude of "why can't I have what my parents have" without realizing that it took the parents years of hard work and saving to have the luxuries and comforts they have now.

Couples in Adele and Joe's era expected to make sacrifices in their early marriages as part of life. Today's baby-boomer couples make personal fulfillment and personal satisfaction a priority and are inflexible and unwilling to wait and make sacrifices for financial rewards in the future.

Looking at the more positive side of family life today, many grandmothers envy the opportunities that their daughters and granddaughters have today. They see them having more self respect, more self confidence and more independence than they had at that age. They have a tinge of jealousy at the opportunity their daughters and granddaughters have of going to college and having careers, but they don't envy young working mothers going to the office eight hours a day, picking up their children at the day care center at day's end, keeping a home and parenting as well.

Writing in 1998, Finnegan Alford Cooper, an anthropologist and author, observed, "Spouses who think times have changed said they socialized their children to different attitudes towards personal fulfillment and sacrifice. In seeking to give children what they didn't have themselves, they created different children from themselves. Not only are attitudes and values different but they recognize that, lack of struggle meant, that the children didn't learn to work hard or why work was important. In centering their lives totally on their children they raised self-centered children."

The reality is that we cannot turn back the clock to 1938. We need to address the marriage situation because, unfortunately, many couples today see it as a legal contract between two people that can be broken by one or both of the parties. We are dealing with a culture where most middle class women have higher education and are gainfully employed, which not only changes the culture of the work place, but also the character of home life as well.

We are also a disposable society living in an age where every thing is created for obsolescence. When I took my bicycle to the repair shop last week, they didn't fix the puncture in my tube with an adhesive patch. They discarded the tube and replaced it with a new one and so it goes sometimes with the contract of marriage.

For couples, young or old, I recommend developing an attitude of a willingness to give more than one receives. To develop such an approach, I refer you back to the chapter where each of you think of doing several things weekly to make living with you in marriage more fun. It could be something as simple as buying tulips for $7.99 a bunch or calling your in-laws once a month just to say "Hi."

Every woman, no matter how secure she is, needs a sign of affection daily. I ask you how much energy does it take to say daily, "Honey, I love you" or, to get up of the couch when she gets home from work and plant a nice kiss on her lips. Next I recommend that you give your spouse space to grow and encouragement to pursue a career that she or he desires.

I unabashedly tell husbands who are extroverts like me, not to flirt with another friend's wife even if she is encouraging you to do so. I have experienced such a situation where one of my wife's colleagues thought it very humorous to flirt with me. I gladly accepted my wife's recommendation that we delete such a couple from our association list.

Somewhere in the first year of marriage, when you are having your one-on-one review as to how the marriage is doing, both parties should make a commitment to each other never to think of calling a divorce lawyer without first seeking counseling from a competent and respected marriage counselor. Even if you are the guilty one, you have the right to appropriate help. This recommendation is not necessary for couples like Joe and Adele, since divorce was never an option even if their relationship stunk.

I advise all couples, whether newly engaged or married 40 years, that when a conflict arises and before the argument becomes too heated, they should learn to withdraw and cool off, think for a little and come up with a compromise.

Learn to distinguish sex from love and be conscious of each other's sexual needs. Traditionally we think of men having the strongest sexual desires. A review of Masters and Johnson's research on the whole subject of sexuality reveals otherwise and my own experience as a marriage counselor confirms that many women have a strong sexual desire throughout their whole marriage and sometimes seek sex more aggressively and more frequently than their husband. If the communication between husband and wife is open and non-judgmental, there is no limit to the joy and fulfillment that couples get from their love life.

I sometimes surprise my clients when I tell them that one vital step to making your marriage grow and last 50 years is taking the time and interest to show respect and affection for your spouse's parents, especially as they grow older. This has been a very fulfilling task for me because Laurie has always been very loving towards her parents and they have always been very responsive to my acts of affection.

I jokingly tell Laurie that the love and attention she shows her parents is a rehearsal for what she will have to do for me in a few years. She just flashes her contagious smile and says, "Don't you know, I have thought of that situation already!"

Epilogue

Recently while I was peddling my book *A Kid From Legaginney* at an Irish festival in Dover, New Hampshire, a lady who had already bought a copy of the book asked, "Finbarr, what is the title of your next book?"

I answered without any hesitation, "*Living, Laughing and Loving thru Marriage.*"

She and her two girlfriends laughed hysterically as she retorted "Is that a joke?" and then went off without telling me why they were laughing. It got me thinking that maybe, not just maybe, but "Yes, I am very lucky to have a marriage where I laugh a lot, love and am loved while living on God's second heaven Cape Cod."

Looking back, I see my life a series of bridges to be crossed, not alone, but with the help of significant people who believed in me and helped me to believe in myself. Even if you marry a saint - and most of us didn't - you are not going to be happy unless you first like yourself and accept yourself "warts and all" as the Creator made you. You are never going to be happy in marriage if you expect your spouse to change and see life exactly as you do.

I got a big laugh out of Laurie one day when I commented, "If I had married someone like myself, an extrovert with all of my idiosyncrasies, I would go crazy, because there would never be enough time for the two of us to hold a conversation." God made my spouse and me different, but complementary.

All we children of God are the work of His hands, shaped in an image, not perfect but placed on this earth for a moment in this world's history to share his gifts of living, laughing and loving. Now I just wish He would tell me what he wants me to do when I really grow up!!!

References

Lisa Cahill, Theologian. *Sex, Gender and Christian Ethics.* [New Studies in Christian Ethics, University Press, Cambridge, Reprinted 2000].

Sidney Callahan, Psychologist and Moral Theologian. *Dissent and the Future of the Catholic Church.*

Reverend George A. Kelly. *The Catholic Marriage Manual.* [Random House New York, 1959].

Pope John Paul 11. *Morality of Marriage.* Public Address, February 11, 1984.

Gail Risch, Researcher, The Creighton Center for Marriage and Family Publication. *Marriage in the Catholic Tradition* [New York, Crossroad Publishing Co., 2004].

Ira Reiss, *Toward a Sociology of Heterosexual Love Relationship* [Marriage and Family Living, May 1960 edition].

Robert T. Francoeur, Sociologist and Author. *Becoming a Sexual Person* [John Wiley & Sons 1982].

Leo F. Buscaglia, Author and Lecturer. *Living, Laughing and Learning* [Ballantine Books, 1985].

Ellen Gallinsky, President and Co-Founder of' Families and Work Institute. *Ask the Children* [1999]. Co-Author of *The National Study of the Changing Workplace.*

Neill S. Jacobson, Professor, Author and Lecturer. Died unexpectedly of an apparent heart attack at age 50, while preparing to participate in a workshop in Las Vegas on Domestic Violence [1999]

Ruth K. Westheimer, Ed.D., Sex Therapist and Author. *Dr. Ruth's Guide for Married Lovers,* [Warner Bros., 1986]. *Sex for Dummies* [IDG Books Worldwide, 1996].

The Palm Beach Post. Article on Parenting, March 16th 2006.